CYBER CRIME

How to Protect Yourself from COMPUTER CRIMINALS

by Laura E. Quarantiello

LIMELIGHT
BOOKS

Book design: John C. Herkimer,
Next Wave Graphics,
Caledonia, NY.

Published by LimeLight Books,
a division of Tiare Publications,
P.O. Box 493, Lake Geneva, WI 53147

ISBN: 0-936653-74-4
Printed in the United States of America.

Library of Congress Cataloging-in-Publication Data

Quarantiello, Laura E., 1968-
    Cyber crime : how to protect yourself from computer criminals / by
Laura E. Quarantiello.
        p.   cm.
    ISBN 0-936653-74-4
    1. Computer crimes.   2. Computer crimes--Prevention.   3. Computer
security.   I. Title.
HV6773.Q37   1996
364.1'68--dc20
                                                        96-22863
                                                           CIP

Table of Contents

ACKNOWLEDGEMENTS 5

ABOUT THIS BOOK 7

PREFACE 9

INTRODUCTION: THE WILD WEST
OF THE ELECTRONIC FRONTIER 11

PART ONE: CRIME ON LINE

INSIDE COMPUTER CRIME
What Is Computer-Related Crime? 16
Computer Criminals: Who Are These Guys, Anyway? 16
Why do Hackers Hack? 21

COMPUTER CRIMINALS AND THEIR CRIMES: DIGITAL OUTLAWS
Phreaking: Misleading Ma Bell and Her Sisters 24
Tools of the Trade 25
Hacking: Online Mayhem 32
Hacking From Within 42

CYBER SNEEZES: VIRUSES
The Common Cold: Types of Viruses 48
Ah-choo! Catching a Virus 50
Damage Assessment: What a Virus Can Do 52
Those Nasty Bugs 52

THE DARKEST SIDE OF COMPUTER CRIME: THREATS TO YOUR
PERSONAL SAFETY AND SECURITY
Crime Online 56
Guess Who? 57

Footsteps Among the Bytes: Online Harassment
and Stalking 59
What's Your Name? Computer Pedophiles
and Pornography 64
Online Pornography 68
Old Crime, New Twist: Fraud 71
Too Close for Comfort: Invasion of Privacy 74

PART TWO: CYBER SECURITY
FOILING COMPUTER CRIMINALS AND STAYING SAFE

LINK 1 - THE HUMAN FACTOR 80
LINK 2 - SYSTEM SECURITY 81
Log-On Procedures 83
Securing Data From Theft 88
Guarding Against Data Manipulation 90
Protection Against Viruses 91
LINK 3: PERSONAL SECURITY 94
Information Dissemination 95
Identity Hoaxes 96
Online Harassment and Stalking 99
Protecting Children Online 99
Maintaining Privacy 101
E-Mail Security 103
LINK 4: PHYSICAL SECURITY 106
Physical Access Controls 106
Site Hardening 108
CYBER COPS: WALKING THE DIGITAL BEAT
Policing the Info Highway 115
Reporting Computer Crime 117
CLOSING THOUGHTS 121
APPENDIX
Resources For More Information 123
CERT Coordination Center Incident Reporting Form 127
Online Resources 133
Glossary 135

Acknowledgements

From the ground up this book has been driven, helped along and eventually produced with the help of a computer. The topic itself was hatched during an online chat, research was done primarily with bulletin board system databases and files and electronic access to various forums and agencies. Information was collected via electronic mail, then stored and read on disk. The actual text of the book was written with WordPerfect 5.0 on a Packard Bell Pentium 100. Paradoxically, this book will do the most good not as words on a computer screen, but in hard-copy form in the hands of computer users.

My thanks go out to the following individuals, organizations and agencies who were, and continue to be, invaluable friends and resources:

David Boyle, former sysop of Dream Net BBS, who helped me decide to write this book;

"Dr. Who" of Lycaeum BBS, who allowed me to troll his alternative bulletin board for information and research;

Will Spencer ("Voyager"), who granted me permission to reprint information from his file of Frequency Asked Questions (FAQs) about hacking, and helped educate me on the nuts and bolts of system access and;

The numerous hackers and phreaks who trusted me enough to talk with me.

My unending appreciation goes to the staff of the City of San Marcos Library for accommodating my numerous requests for inter-library loans.

Sincere thanks to Pete Romfh of AT&T for a great collection of hacker-related periodicals and files which helped me to understand the mentality of the computer underground, and for his help with the manuscript;

Special Agent Michael R. Anderson with the Internal Revenue Service's Criminal Investigations Division for going out of his way to provide me with information on current issues and news about cyber security, as well as for his critique of the manuscript;

Michael E. Chesbro for help with computer security resources;

David Kennedy, United States Army Military Police (Information Systems Security) for taking the time to expound on points for clarification;

John Bailey for providing his expertise on privacy issues;

Special Agent Dave Messinger, IRS-CID); and

Dr. Gerald L. Kovacich, Information Security Management Associates, for their critiques of the manuscript.

A tip of the cyber cap to my friends on both the CompuServe Crime Forum and Author's Forum for assistance, support, encouragement and for providing a second home.

Thanks also to the following organizations and personnel for invaluable technical information:

National Computer Security Association (NCSA), especially Jonathan Wheat;

United States Department of Commerce, National Institute of Standards and Technology (NIST), Computer Systems Laboratory, especially Dianne Ward;

Federal Bureau of Investigation (FBI), Computer Analysis and Response Team, Washington, DC;

United States Secret Service (USSS), Electronic Crimes Branch, Washington, DC;

National Computer Security Center, INFOSEC Awareness Division, Ft. George G. Meade, Maryland;

Computer Emergency Response Team (CERT), Coordination Center, Carnegie Mellon University, Pittsburgh, Pennsylvania.

Abundant thanks to Gerry Dexter of Tiare Publications for his confidence in me and his hard work on my behalf.

Special thanks to my family who have come to understand that when I'm sitting in front of a computer screen, no matter what it may look like, I really *am* working!

- *Laura E. Quarantiello*

About this Book

This book is about crime and computers. It is a walk through the dark areas of cyberspace; a look at some of the negative things you may encounter in the computer world. There can be no question that the advantages of computers, the pluses, far outweigh the minuses. I know because I have been a computer user for years and I've seen and experienced the good. Unfortunately, I've also seen some of the bad. Computer crime is very real, never mind that it amounts to only a small portion of the whole.

Whenever we talk about crime in any area, we run the risk of being labeled an alarmist. This book is not meant to alarm you; it is meant to inform you and make you aware of some of the dangers you might encounter. Today's computer systems are very vulnerable to attack and, as Frederick B. Cohen, Ph.D, a pioneer in the field of computer viruses said, the threat should not be minimized. I'd like to take the conservative road and say that unless you work for a government agency, large corporation or industry, your chances of becoming a victim of a computer-related crime are low, but I cannot say that. It wouldn't be true.

Computers have become such a vital part of daily life that the possibility exists that, whoever you are, wherever you work, you may encounter the negative side of computers and computing. As long as such a possibility exists there is a real need for a book such as this one.

This book is not intended to be a comprehensive text on computer security. Books like those, running to several hundred pages, seldom make it off the bookstore shelves and into the hands of the everyday, average computer user. Even when they do, most readers don't get past the first chapter.

Instead, this book is intended to be a fast and easy handbook discussing what the threats to our computers are and explaining the steps you can take toward countering them. It is intended to educate you and give you information you can put to immediate use to safeguard your computers and your computer activities in both your home and business, without first having to become a computer wizard. Read it, use it, and be safe.

DISCLAIMER

The information contained in this book is designed solely for informational purposes; every attempt has been made to ensure that the contents are accurate, but no responsibility will be accepted, by either the author or the publisher, for actions or incidents resulting from or through use of the information presented herein.

Preface

I'm not a hacker but I know a few and I know some of the police officers who chase them. I've lurked in the electronic shadows, beyond the binary curve and I've listened to both sides talk - some in whispers, others in shouts.

I've listened to hackers talk about connecting with a main-frame computer somewhere in another area code, maybe even in another country, slipping past the log-on screen, tip-toeing around the security set up and plunging into places they don't belong, doing things they shouldn't do. I've been amused by their sense of humor, their way with words, their smug attitudes and their zest for all things electronic. I've shaken my head, even winced at the descriptions of their antics in the cyber realm, some beyond the fringes of legality. Some are programmers, "true" hackers. Some are troublemakers; anti-establishment revolution-aries. Regardless, I've found myself actually liking some of these people, who are only "handles" on a monitor screen; people I've never met and probably never will.

I've listened to police officers talk about a fix for the latest trap door that some hacker discovered, about setting up a "sting board," about the wild ethics hackers claim to have. I've listened to them lament a bureaucracy that relegates cyber crimes to the basement and a justice system that is slow to understand and properly prosecute computer-related crime.

Some of these officers were street cops (some still are), pulled in from the beat simply because they happened to know some-thing about computers. Some are detectives, struggling with search and seizure laws that sometimes seem to defy the rules of evidence, because computer data isn't tangible like a gun or a knife. Most of them are overwhelmed with fighting traditional crime, and deep in their souls they are horrified that the fight against crime goes on as fiercely as ever, only in a different form. I like these people, too. And I respect them.

The people I know best, those I identify with and can say that I'm one of, are the garden-variety computer users. They use their computers for business or for entertainment, at work and at home. They make up the great majority of computer users and their lives are connected, somehow, in some way, to cyberspace.

More join the ranks every day, wiring into the Net, going online, exploring and learning in a new land. They don't know hackers, they don't know cops, they don't know that crime occasionally travels the information superhighway. If they get hit from behind by a runaway big rig on the infobahn they will learn of these things and finally realize how vulnerable they are. I don't want them to learn that way, as a casualty of a reckless keyboard artist. I want them to walk with awareness in cyberspace, protecting themselves against hackers, stalkers, viruses and all the other virtual threats which exist out there in the ether. I want the everyday, garden variety computer user to be safe, as I have learned to be safe in this place called cyberspace.

This book, then, is for computer users everywhere and for those who fight against computer crime. It is my sincere hope that it will contribute to making your life in cyberspace safer and law enforcement's job easier.

INTRODUCTION

The Wild West of the Electronic Frontier

> *"Computing is not about computers anymore, it is about living."*
>
> - Nicholas Negroponte
> MIT Media Lab

There is a place called cyberspace. It is a parallel universe of sorts, a place which exists both within this world and in some undefinable area out beyond it. People have been visiting this place for years, connecting with it each time they lifted a handset to talk with someone at the other end of a telephone line, used an automatic teller machine or stood in a supermarket check-out line and watched their groceries being scanned across a bar code reader. Perhaps they didn't know that this place had a name. But it has.

The relentless march of time and technology has carried more and more of us into cyberspace. Not only can we travel there by telephone, but by facsimile machine and radio. And by computer. In fact, the computer has allowed us to do something in cyberspace that we had never been able to accomplish in this place before: create a community.

The cyberspace community has no physical dimensions and no tangible barriers. Yet people go there to talk, play, work, exchange information, leave messages and interact. They go to this place from all points of the globe, arriving in a microsecond, zipping along a coaxial or fiber-optic cable.

You cannot walk to cyberspace, but you can reach it. You cannot touch cyberspace, but it can be occupied. In fact, if you were to try to reach out and touch cyberspace it's likely you would experience the shock of 120 volts straight-filtered through wires and circuit boards. Cyberspace can't be touched with the human hand. This community can only be reached through a telephone line and a computer keyboard.

The virtual community of cyberspace is peopled by adults and children, men and women, white collar and blue collar, rich and poor. You cannot distinguish social classes in cyberspace, and so there are none. You cannot ascertain race or religion unless someone volunteers the information, and so these things are usually of little importance. Unless your system is equipped with the ultimate in high tech you cannot see or hear other people. Other than those differences, cyberspace is a fairly typical pseudo-universe.

It has areas where business is conducted, places where entertainment may be enjoyed, where keyboard conversations can take place, and work can be done. It has educators, bankers, businessmen, physicians, attorneys, aviators, military officers, secretaries, homemakers, and people from every other profession imaginable.

There are friendships in cyberspace and groups which meet regularly to discuss (or cuss) any topic you can think of. There is torrid romance, there are heated arguments. There is enraged shouting, harmless teasing, good-natured joking and even some crying. There are neighborhoods, businesses and "homes." From the comfort of your armchair you can experience in cyberspace most of what you do in your everyday life. You can practically live in cyberspace, with all its strengths and foibles.

But, like any other community - virtual or real - cyberspace is not perfect. You can get hurt there. You can be threatened, attacked, harassed, robbed. There is crime in this new community, committed by criminals you cannot see, rarely hear from and may never even realize had been doing their thing until it is too late. The offenses they commit in this virtual universe are much the same as those they commit in the real world: theft, fraud, larceny, extortion, embezzlement, espionage, tampering, forgery, sabotage, piracy, smuggling, terrorism, pornography, pedophilia, impersonation, invasion of privacy, assault - even attempted murder.

In the virtual back alleys of cyberspace you can be ambushed by modern day criminals: phreakers, hackers, cyberpunks, cypherpunks, virus writers, information warriors, techno-anarchists and techno-bandits. These outlaws ride their computer keyboards into the wildest West imaginable, a place that, in most cases, has few restraints and even fewer laws. They may be as dangerous in their world as a doped-up carjacker with a 9mm handgun is in ours.

High-tech terrorism online is the fastest-growing type of crime. Law enforcement is unable to give us statistics on this form of crime because it is so elusive and so many people don't even report their victimization out of embarrassment, fear or simple ignorance. We can begin to judge the scope of the problem, however, by looking at related statistics.

There are an estimated 110 million personal computers in use throughout the world. In 1994 alone, 48 million personal computers were sold in the United States. Thirty-three percent of all U.S. households have a personal computer. As for the rest, undoubtedly someone in them will encounter and use computers at work, simply because the top occupations in the United States are administrative support positions such as secretarial, professional, executive, or managerial. The majority of these occupations make use of computers. In fact, a survey conducted by Microsoft and IntelliQuest revealed that almost 87 percent of Americans believe that someday all work will involve computers.

We are looking at a world rapidly entering cyberspace. What we find there, behind the blinking cursor and luminescent screen, is a frontier not unlike the one our ancestors found as they traveled west with their wagons.

This electronic frontier is a land that is foreign, exciting, limitless and occasionally dangerous. This wild West is still developing and growing. As it grows, it will mature, but, to some degree at least, it will always be a dangerous place. Anyone who travels there must be prepared to face the possible threats from the outlaws hiding out in the virtual hills. If you believe you cannot be harmed in this place, then you are a victim-in-waiting. Our ancestors were aware of the dangers that might be waiting for them and most of them survived to tame the frontier and turn it into a land where people could thrive. As settlers of the electronic frontier, we need to use some of that old fashioned common sense. It's time to circle the wagons and defend ourselves from cyber crime.

PART ONE

Terrorism On Line:
Inside Computer Crime

"Crime involving high-technology is going to go off the boards."

- Special Agent William Tafoya
Federal Bureau of Investigation

Our increasingly high-tech world is a jungle of cables, wires, cords, input/output lines, circuit boards, chattering printers, humming hard disks, and tapping keys. These sights and sounds remind us that there is no way around this technological maze; all of us are or will be forced to make friends with it as it encroaches even more deeply into our daily lives. And so we do our bookkeeping with a computer spreadsheet program, we send electronic mail instead of written letters, we use an automatic teller machine at the bank, sign our names on the pressure-sensitive area of a United Parcel Service computerized clipboard, search for a book title on the local library's electronic card catalog, check for medication interactions with the pharmacy's computer system. Without our even realizing it, computers have become an integral part of our daily routine. Even if we refuse to have a personal computer in our home, we find that we cannot avoid them totally; they pop up elsewhere like persistent weeds. And if we cannot avoid computers, then we have to be concerned over the possibility of becoming a victim of computer-related crime.

"The worst myth, the basis of most others, is that computer crime is a technologists' problem. In reality, computer crime victimizes us all," wrote Buck BloomBecker in his book *Spectacular Computer Crimes*. Everyone is at risk to some degree. If it isn't gangsters with guns making us afraid to step out of the door, it's criminals with keyboards making us wary of flipping the power switch on our PC's. Welcome to the jungle.

WHAT IS COMPUTER-RELATED CRIME?

Computer-related crime is formally defined as any illegal act in which knowledge of computer technology is used to commit the offense. There are four main categories which are recognized for the purposes of threat assessment, risk reduction and intrusion protection:

- Unauthorized use of computer-related assets.
- Introduction of fraudulent records or data into a computer system.
- Alteration or destruction of information or files.
- Theft, by electronic means or otherwise, of money, financial instruments, property, services or data.

Computer-related crime can be perpetrated internally, by employees or persons with legitimate access to individual computers or networks, or externally by unauthorized persons dialing in through a telephone line that accesses a system or network. Both internal and external methods of penetration expose computer systems to the four categories of computer-related crime described above.

COMPUTER CRIMINALS:
WHO ARE THESE GUYS, ANYWAY?

The public and the mass media have bestowed the name "hacker" on anyone who enters a computer system illegally, or uses a computer to commit a crime. In reality, the term hacker isn't so easily defined. It is far more all-encompassing.

The arcane art of exploring computer systems to see how things work began in the early 1970's among computer programmers at the

Massachusetts Institute of Technology, and the computer science and electrical engineering departments of various other universities. The only goal these people were concerned with was to explore the inner workings of computers and learn how they could be manipulated, altered, modified or broken.

These guys were the first true hackers, "poke and probe" fellows, hardware gurus and software experts who were out to learn as much about computers as possible. Their basic philosophy was to take nothing, break nothing, and learn everything. That was their code and they lived by it. They loved the challenge of circumventing layers of security measures, gaining access and going as deeply into the innards of a system as possible, looking around and then departing. They believed they had the right to do this simply because they had the ability to do so. They had no intention of doing harm to the system and, in fact, would often leave an anonymous message for the system administrator, pointing out the deficiencies in the program which had allowed them to gain access.

Hacking systems was seen as an honorable undertaking, perpetrated in the name of education, and causing no damage. But for some it soon went beyond innocent exploring and degenerated into outright intrusion. It was at this point that the terms "hacking" and "hacker" began to take on negative connotations among the public. No longer was a hacker just a student innocently fooling around with his computer, or a programmer learning the intricacies of a system: now he was a criminal.

Well-publicized cases such as the arrest of members of Milwaukee's 414 Gang - who broke into computers belonging to the Los Alamos National Laboratory in New Mexico and the Memorial Sloan Kettering Cancer Center in New York City - and the release of the movie *War Games*, changed the direction of hacking forever.

At this point hacking philosophy split. There were still hackers who were in the game only to explore systems and do no harm. They still exist, still living by the code of conduct that keeps them on the legal side of the line. This type of hacker should properly be called a computer guru, but some diehards are reluctant to let the term hacker go and so the semantical argument goes on.

The second type of hacker let his technical knowledge, his unrestrained curiosity and marginal morals lead him straight across the line between the legal and illegal. He became what everyone popularly thought the word hacker meant: a malicious type who broke into computer systems, destroyed data, stole files and used networks for his own personal, illicit gain. Some call this criminal a "cracker."

With the birth of the malicious hacker came the beginning of a culture sociologists and law enforcement officers have come to call the computer underground. The underground is said to be peopled by those who use computers to engage in illegal activities such as hacking, phreaking and to a lesser extent, software pirating. The line between hackers and phreaks is somewhat blurred today, but generally phreaks are primarily interested in manipulating the telephone system to avoid charges, while hackers are interested in exploring and exploiting computer systems. Telecommunications networks are now run almost exclusively by computers, so phreaks and hackers tend to associate because of the similarities in their activities. Somewhere between the two is the pirating, or illegal copying, of copyrighted computer software.

Many of these people - hackers and phreaks - walk the fringe between legal and illegal, in that area ruled only by personal ethics, where right and wrong is a matter of degree. Bruce V. Bigelow, writing in the *San Diego Union-Tribune*, put it this way: "Conventional notions of right and wrong seem to go fuzzy in the ethereal realm that hackers call cyberspace." Most hackers believe that government and industry have a stranglehold over the public and therefore all information should remain free.

In a paper presented at the 1990 National Computer Security Conference, Dorothy Denning, Professor of Computer Science at Georgetown University, said her findings led her to conclude that hacking "belongs at the very least to the gray areas between larger conflicts that we are experiencing at every level of society and business, the conflict between the idea that information cannot be owned and the idea that it can, and the conflict between law enforcement and the First and Fourth Amendments."

Many hackers conclude that breaking into a system is not morally wrong as long as no damage is done. The definition of damage varies: a hacker may define damage as crashing a system, deleting files or planting viruses, while law enforcement may define damage as the mere act of gaining access without authorization, reading files, downloading files, and using computer time or tying up system resources.

Donn B. Parker of SRI International, a computer security think tank, describes many hackers and phreaks as having the Robin Hood Syndrome. They maintain that harming individual people is immoral, but harming an organization, a computer system or the data in a computer is acceptable behavior. "If I can get into your system, then whatever I find on it is fair game. The fault lies with you, for not having adequate security," said one hacker.

By their own admission, hackers believe that they live outside the normal rules that govern our society. This feeling of freedom has had a profound effect on many hackers, producing warped and twisted ethics. These "ethics" are those of a culture on the edge, swinging out of control. This so-called counterculture may prove to be more damaging than we think; only time will tell that tale.

Beyond the fringe lies the truly illegal, the basic core criminal whose intention from the beginning is to commit a crime. AT&T Engineer Pete Romfh says "these guys generally aren't hackers, they are crooks who use hacking techniques just like they use a gun or a set of lockpicks." It isn't a game to them, or fun, or a right. It's pure crime and it has nothing to do with rights and freedoms. "The modern thief can steal more with a computer than with a gun," according to the National Research Council. Today, you may well find the modern criminal toting a laptop instead of a handgun. It's safer, quicker and there is less fear of getting caught.

What we have, then, is the good, the bad and the ugly: the innocent hacker, the fringe hacker and the criminal hacker. They all exist, but in numbers we cannot estimate. Do fringe hackers outweigh criminal hackers? Do innocent hackers dominate fringe hackers? We simply don't know the percentages because we don't know the extent of the intrusions.

A Department of Justice official, testifying before a United States Senate committee, stated that "computer crime is a low-visibility proposition. There are no smoking pistols, no blood-stained victims; often the crime is detected by sheer accident." We know they are out there, tapping on keyboards, making modem connections, but we may never see them in our systems. Only later, when the damage - however minor - is done, will we realize an intrusion has occurred. Michel E. Kabay, Ph.D., Director of Education for the National Computer Security Association (NCSA) said, "In statistical parlance, we are basing our estimates of the computer criminal population on a biased sample: the ones we know about. What about all the ones we don't know about?"

We may be hazy on how many hackers there are, but we aren't hazy on their common characteristics. Law enforcement officers and clinical psychologists who study the subject have determined that computer criminals usually possess similar attributes. They are generally young, but may be anywhere from 15 to 45 years of age. They possess high level skills and knowledge of technical subjects. They are not necessarily above average students, but they may possess above average intellect. They are commonly amateurs, not professional criminals. Hackers are predominantly male, although females have been involved in several known cases and cannot be ruled out of the equation. A 1988 survey by the National Center for Computer Crime Data revealed that in California 32 percent of persons arrested for computer crime were women, 43 percent were minorities and 25 percent were white males.

If employed, it will be in a position of trust within a company or business, such as a clerk, programmer, or system manager having legitimate access to data processing systems. They usually work alone, but in order to commit some crimes they may need the assistance of others to obtain access numbers, passwords, log-on codes or other information not readily at hand. Usually they have no previous law enforcement record.

"Most of the news stories I read simplify the problem to the point of saying that a hacker is a hacker is a hacker," said SRI's Donn Parker. "In real life, what we're dealing with is a very broad spectrum of individuals. It goes all the way from 14-year olds playing pranks on their friends to hardened juvenile delinquents, career criminals and international terrorists."

WHY DO HACKERS HACK?

As a general rule, hackers love a challenge and are fascinated by the minutiae of computer technology. It is often this fascination that takes them over the edge and into committing crimes - some minor, some major - via computer. Dr. Percy Black, Professor of Psychology at New York's Pace University says hackers may all share a common search for a feeling of power, possibly stemming from a deep-seated sense of powerlessness. Acts of computer-related crime serve as over-compensation for feelings of inferiority. The apparent immaturity of the hacker, according to Dr. Black, may be the expression of unresolved feelings of resentment and powerlessness that all of us must overcome as we mature. A common quote cited by hackers is "knowledge is power," a statement attributed to 17th century English philosopher-statesman Francis Bacon. Knowledge is, indeed, the ultimate power. And nowhere is power more readily available than through the thousands of databases and systems accessible by computer.

Hackers may also be seeking the supreme high, a peak experience that they are unable to achieve with any other activity. Dr. Black believes that the anti-social behavior of hackers may be related to inadequate endogenous stimulation, resulting in an abnormally high need for such inner stimulation. This inadequacy leads to unacceptable acts that serve to alleviate the demand.

Some behavioral scientists believe that many hackers suffer from a computer addiction, similar to drug or alcohol dependence. Once hooked, the preoccupation with hacking systems isn't easy to control. The obsession can drive hackers to forgo food and sleep as they plunge deeper and deeper into a system's maze.

Ask a hacker why he hacks and he may well say, "because I can." This is true for the innocent hacker as well as the criminal hacker. Technology has given the gift of access to the computer-capable; just beyond the log-on prompt sits everything from information to money. The person who can get into the system and manipulate the program may be able to have it all - for free. He may just want to copy a program or a file, or he may want to funnel funds from different accounts to his own. Or, he may simply want to browse around.

Emmanuel Goldstein, editor of *2600: The Hacker Quarterly* testified before a Congressional subcommittee in 1993, saying: "I think the common bond that we all have is curiosity, an intense form of curiosity, something that in many cases exceeds the limitations that many of us would like to put on curiosity. The thing is though, you cannot really put a limitation on curiosity..."

Once into a system, the line between the law abiding and the criminal can become thin: it all comes down to the ethics of the person tapping away at the keyboard.

What motivates a hacker to do more than just innocently browse someone else's system? The main motivations are fairly straightforward and easily defined. Breaching a system may be done for recreation, to test the limits of technology, to commit malicious attacks on corporations, businesses or societies, to attain revenge against employers, co-workers and other individuals or to gain personal profit. In the end, it all comes down to one or more of those six reasons.

Computer Criminals and Their Crimes: Digital Outlaws

> *"Today, there is virtually no system or network, either telecommunications or mainframe computer, that has not been compromised...A new breed of criminal is emerging and unfortunately appears to be here to stay. You can be sure that they are out there right now trying to crack your system!"*
>
> - Michel E. Kabay, Ph.D
>   National Computer Security Association

The visible enemy has always been the easiest to fight: he is flesh and blood standing before us. But the invisible enemy is a tougher opponent. How can we defend ourselves against an enemy that lurks in shadows, behind a keyboard, at the far end of a fiber-optic telephone line? How can you possibly fight back against the unknown?

If you know the enemy's intent and the way he does battle you can begin to defend against him. As Sun Tzu advised in *The Art of War*: "Therefore, determine the enemy's plans and you will know which strategy will be successful and which will not." The first step in defending against computer criminals is understanding the crimes they commit.

PHREAKING: MISLEADING MA BELL
AND HER SISTERS

There was a time when the act of lifting the handset of your telephone opened a relay, lit up a tiny electric line lamp and put you in direct contact with a live human being - a telephone operator - instead of today's impersonal dial tone. The operator, with her cords and jacks, *was* the telephone system; without her you couldn't talk to anyone, local or long distance. But you could listen. You could always listen, simply by lifting the handset while another conversation was taking place.

As telephones became more popular and their use spread throughout the country, telephone operators found it increasingly difficult to handle the load of incoming calls by switching them manually. Service slowed due to the increased demand. So the telephone company began to automate the switching system, using electro-mechanical switches and relays controlled by dialed digits. Telephone signals from home or office were carried over a local "loop" - a pair of copper wires - to the local central switching office, where they were connected to a switching machine. This eased the pressure on human operators, but it was a cumbersome, maintenance-heavy affair. It also threw a roadblock in the way of those busy-bodies who liked to eavesdrop on conversations.

In the latter half of the 1950's, AT&T implemented a revolutionary new idea it called Direct Long Distance Dialing, or DDD. DDD allowed customers to make unassisted calls to places like Phoenix, Peru or Pago Pago, connecting to far-off cities and lands just by dialing a set of numbers on their home telephone. A series of rapid, audible tones sent switching and billing information through the system, enabling a connection to take place automatically, without the intervention of an operator. If you listen closely, these tones can still be heard as faint echoes following a dialing string on systems that use in-band signaling instead of the newer ESS (Electronic Signaling System).

With the introduction of high-speed computers to handle call switching, a new opportunity for meddling presented itself. You couldn't fool a live operator, but a computer was another story.

In September, 1970, a fellow named John Draper discovered that by blowing the whistle he'd gotten as a prize in a "Cap'n Crunch" cereal box, he could reproduce the 2600 Hertz in-band signaling tone which sent billing information over a local line to the telephone company's main office computer. In effect, Draper could seize control of a telephone line simply by using the whistle to fool the computer into thinking that he was a telephone operator!

The whistle, and later, specially-built "Blue Boxes" which created multi-frequency tones, allowed users to access special switch functions normally available only to telephone company employees. The switches allowed the circumventing of long-distance charges, free conference calling and other goodies. So was born the practice known as phone phreaking. Those who engage in it are known as phreakers or phone phreaks, and they continue to assault the telephone system with their tricks and techniques.

TOOLS OF THE TRADE

Cheating the telephone company has become a sort of game, a way to beat the faceless, behind-the-times, foot-dragging system that phone phreaks are convinced is a menace to society. The easiest way to obtain free service - which is the ultimate goal of any phone phreak - is to use someone else's long distance access code.

Bruce Sterling, author of *The Hacker Crackdown* calls this level of phreaking "pig easy...requiring practically no expertise." In fact, anyone can do it. Simply stand by a bank of pay phones in an airport concourse, a mall or hotel lobby and watch callers punch in their codes. This type of phreaking, known as "shoulder surfing," requires only that you be discreet and have a good head for remembering a string of numbers. In fact, some phreakers are so adept they can memorize the pattern your finger traces on the ten-digit phone pad and then repeat your moves. The monetary losses to this type of crime are enormous, and they grow exponentially each time a phone access code is posted on a computer bulletin board, traded or sold to other phreaks. If you're the unlucky citizen who happened to have your code shoulder-surfed you probably won't know about it until you read the heart-stopping bottom line on your next phone bill.

Although shoulder surfing is the easiest way to obtain phone codes, it isn't the only method used. Once phone phreaks discovered the power of the computer, they found that it was a simple matter to write a program that would repeatedly dial combinations of numbers until it hit on one that worked. More sophisticated programs would log the number and continue trying others, racking up a list of useable codes. This practice still has some merit today, but it can be detected by the telephone company and by law enforcement agencies, so it is usually left to amateurs to dabble in.

Phreaks quickly found that the computers which controlled the telephone system were fair game and could be fooled. So they began to devise tools to hack the setup. The Blue Box, mentioned above, has given way to dozens of other types of home-built boxes that play havoc with the phone company and its lines.

The corner pay phone was easily hacked through the use of a Red Box. The Red Box works on the concept of reproducing coin drop tones. Whenever a coin is inserted into a pay phone, the phone emits a set of tones. Using a Red Box, these tones can be simulated, fooling the pay phone into believing that an actual coin has been inserted. Red boxes gained popularity because they were so easy to make: such items as a modified Radio Shack tone dialer, an electronic greeting card, or common electronic components were the heart of the Red Box.

Of course, it didn't stop there. If a tweak to the phone system was dreamed up, hackers built a box to make it work.

Box Name:	What it Does:
Acrylic:	Steals three-way-calling, call-waiting and programmable call-forwarding on old four-wire phone systems.
Aqua:	Drains the voltage of the FBI lock-in-trace/trap-trace.
Beige:	Lineman's handset.
Black:	Avoids billing to the calling party.

Blast:	Phone microphone amplifier.
Blotto:	Supposedly shorts out every phone in the immediate area.
Blue:	Emulates an operator by seizing a trunk via 2600 Hertz (Hz) tone.
Brown:	Creates a party line from two phone lines.
Bud:	Taps into your neighbor's phone line.
Cheese:	Connects two phones to create a diverter.
Chrome:	Manipulates traffic signals by remote control.
Clear:	A telephone pickup coil and a small amp used to make free calls on Fortress Phones.
Color:	Line-activated telephone recorder.
Copper:	Causes crosstalk interference on an extender.
Crimson:	Hold button.
Dark:	Re-routes outgoing or incoming calls to another phone. (Also Diverter.)
Dayglo:	Connects to your neighbor's phone line.
Gold:	Traces calls, tells if the call is being traced, and can change a trace.
Green:	Emulates the Coin Collect, Coin Return, and Ringback tones.
Infinity:	Remotely-activated phone tap.
Jack:	Touch-Tone key pad.
Lunch:	AM transmitter.
Magenta:	Connects a remote phone line to another remote phone line.
Mauve:	Phone tap without cutting into a line.
Neon:	External microphone.
Noise:	Creates line noise.
Olive:	External ringer.

Party:	Creates a party line from two phone lines. (Also Pink.)
Pearl:	Tone generator.
Purple:	Telephone hold button.
Razz:	Taps into your neighbor's phone.
Red:	Generates quarter tones for free pay phone calls.
Rock:	Adds music to your phone line.
Scarlet:	Causes a neighbor's phone line to have poor reception.
Static:	Keeps the voltage on a phone line high.
Switch:	Adds hold, indicator lights, conferencing, etc.
Tan:	Line-activated telephone recorder.
Tron:	Reverses the phase of power to your house, causing your electric meter to run slower.
Urine:	Creates a capacitative disturbance between the ring and tip wires in another's telephone headset.
Violet:	Keeps a pay phone from hanging up.
White:	Portable Dual tone multi-function (DTMF) keypad.
Yellow:	Adds an extension phone.

All of these colored boxes have one thing in common: they trick the phone system into doing something it doesn't normally do for a paying customer. It's sneaky, it's underhanded, but is it wrong? As Bruce Sterling wrote "after all, the long distance lines were just sitting there...Whom did it hurt, really? If you're not damaging the system, and you're not using up any tangible resource, and if nobody finds out what you did, then what real harm have you done?"

Donald P. Delaney, Senior Investigator with the New York State Police explained in a 1993 appearance before Congress that "all telecommunications is controlled by computers. Computer criminals abuse these systems not only for free service but for a variety of crimes ranging from harassment to grand larceny and illegal wiretapping."

A prime example of this is Kevin Lee Poulsen, who used his computer to block incoming telephone lines to three Los Angeles radio stations so that he could be the winning contest caller. Poulsen, a former computer security consultant to the Pentagon, hijacked the phone lines and won two Porsche automobiles from KIIS-FM, $20,000 from KPWR-FM and two trips to Hawaii plus $2,000 from KRTH-FM. He was caught and sentenced to four years in prison.

Anytime you place a computer at the other end of a phone line, you invite trouble. Many businesses today use Voice Mail Systems (VMS) to replace or supplement human receptionists. These are more than just advanced answering machines, they are computers. VMS allows authorized company employees to obtain a voice mailbox, which is capable of receiving and storing messages from callers, sending messages to other boxes on the system, and sending messages to a pre-selected group of boxes. To leave a message, a caller dials the company's 800 or other number and hears a recorded greeting identifying the system, along with instructions for leaving a message. The caller can select from among several options, one of which is to leave a message after the tone.

The message is stored in digitized form by the computer system. An outside caller only needs to know the assigned voice mailbox number (usually two, three or four digits) in order to leave a message for a particular person. To retrieve or delete messages, the person to whom the box is assigned must know not only the box number, but also a confidential password.

Phone phreaks exploit the system by gaining access, changing passwords to deny access to legitimate users and then using the mailboxes for themselves. This VMS abuse usually doesn't cause direct harm to the company which uses it, but it certainly restricts usage by employees and causes unnecessary frustration.

PBXs (Private Branch Exchanges) fall victim to hackers just as frequently as voice mailboxes, the only difference being that the loss can be much greater. A phone phreak who is able to hack into a PBX can then use the PBX to dial back out. The hacker-made calls are almost always long distance and, of course, end up being billed to the company.

Diversion through call-forwarding is another phreaker's trick. A prime example of this is the case of a Philadelphia plumber who used call-forwarding to steal customers from his competitors. Michael Lasch allegedly called the Bell Atlantic Telephone Company and ordered their ultra call-forwarding service for telephones listed in the names of several other plumbing companies. Using the call-forwarding feature, Lasch was able to have calls intended for the other companies forwarded to him. Lasch was charged with theft by deception, criminal attempt, unlawful use of a computer, criminal trespass and impersonating an employee.

The increasing speed at which technology is advancing continues to offer new opportunities for even more phone phreaking. The widespread use of cellular mobile telephones has given phreakers yet another avenue of the phone system to exploit. Technically adept phreaks can reprogram cell phone chips to clone phones and make free calls on someone else's account.

Anytime a cellular phone is on - not engaged in a call, but simply in a ready status to make or receive a call - the phone searches and locks onto the nearest cellular site control channel. As the phone moves through the different cell site areas, the control channel changes and the phone picks up the switch and locks on to the new channel. When a call is made, two pieces of information are transmitted electronically: the caller's 10-digit phone number or Mobile Identification Number (MIN) and the phone's Electronic Serial Number (ESN).

The mobile phone's ESN and MIN are instantly checked against a database of valid access codes at the mobile carrier switch station; if they are not valid the call does not go through. Phone phreaks have found that by recording the electronic data bursts with an ESN Reader (a radio scanner and decoder device) and then reprogramming cellular phones with the access code information, they can create an electronic clone of a legitimate phone and make any type of call they wish: local, long distance, international. "Programming a cloned MIN/ESN into a phone takes only about five minutes," says Todd H. Young, an expert in cellular fraud and director of Consulting Services for the Guidry Group, which specializes in telecommunications security.

Cloned phones are bought and sold by "distributors" in a strange sort of "gray" market in which users may get a week or a month of free calls before the cloned number is discovered and service discontinued. The user simply returns the phone to the distributor, who reprograms it with a new number, and the cycle starts again. Michael R. Guidry, founder and chairman of the Guidry Group, testified before Congress that "what has happened is, those clone devices have been placed in the hands of people that we call ET houses, I guess you would say, and they are the new immigrants that come into the United States for the most part that do not have telephone subscriptions on the land line or on the carrier side from cellular, and now they are charged as much as $25 for 15 minutes to place a call to their home."

Criminals, too, benefit from cloned phones. "Now we have gang members, drug dealers, and gambling, prostitution, vice, just all sorts of crime, stepping forward to use this system where, by using the cloning, they are avoiding law enforcement," noted Guidry. Authorities estimate that stolen air time amounts to over one million dollars per day, as phreaks and other savvy criminals exploit cellular technology.

Yet another toy for phone phreaks to play with are packet switching networks such as TYMNET and TELENET. Once dialed into a local access number, it's only a matter of doing some fancy keyboard work to hack into one of the computers connected to the network. That computer can be in the same city or in a city 7,000 miles away. The cost of the call ends up on the bill of the person's account the phreak used to access the net.

Perhaps the best hacks, the ones that give phreaks the most glee, are those that involve utilizing telephone company internal maintenance switches, which are, for the most part, not public knowledge. One such hack involves loops. Loops are a pair of consecutive phone numbers, such as 865-9998 and 865-9999, which are used by the phone company for testing. To a phone phreak, a loop is a gift from heaven.

One phreak explained that each loop has two ends, called the high end and low end. One of the ends emits a constant, loud tone when it is dialed, while the other end remains silent. When both ends of the loop are called, the people who placed the call at each end can talk through the loop. They enjoy a free phone call, billed to the local phone company.

The art and sport of phone phreaking is considered the predecessor of modern hacking. As soon as phone phreaks discovered the personal computer and began to use it, they crossed the already blurred line between phreaks and hackers. The difference between the two is simply that phreaks are more interested in manipulating the telephone system for their own use and gain, while the hackers are only interested in the computer at the other end of the phone line. Here is where the culture of phreaking breaks off into what may be called a subculture known as computer hacking.

HACKING: ONLINE MAYHEM

The first hackers weren't criminals, they were computer programmers who chose the label of "hacker" because it described exactly what they did, which was to chop, cut, slash, slice and carve computers. Early computer hardware and software products were large, ungainly and plodding, and often had to be tinkered with in order to work properly. This tinkering often led to wholesale surgery when a system went down and refused to come back up.

In the colleges and universities, where cutting edge research was being done in the fields of computer science and artificial intelligence, computer programmers were largely students. Every day they had their minds and hands deep into the guts of a computer, fixing it, tweaking it, forcing it to perform or outperform what it had done the day before. If a program failed to work as advertised, you hacked it. You broke through the security and slipped into the operating code and added or deleted until it did work. If you needed more computing power to run an application - power that, as a lowly student, you weren't allowed access to - you found a trap door into the mainframe and dropped in for a little late night work at two or three times the speed of what they gave you to work with by day. Computer programmers were hackers by necessity, and in humming college computer labs they spawned strange and arcane programs that did things they weren't supposed to do, using computer power they weren't supposed to have.

These early hackers were explorers. They got in and got out, using what they needed, being very careful not to leave any digital footprints which would reveal they had been there. They were voyagers who intended only to learn, to further their education, never to do harm. Some would become leaders of the coming computer revolution, taking computers to the masses, creating the companies that lead the computing profession today.

But for others it was a different story: somewhere along the path - like Adam, Eve and the apple in the Garden of Eden - they were tempted. The temptation called with a voice that said "you can have more: more power, more knowledge, more everything." The password cracking, Trojan Horses and trap door discoveries that allowed them to explore university mainframes could get them into other systems as well; bigger and better systems with more power and more information than the college machines could ever hope to possess. So, filled with heady thoughts of what could be, the programmers hacked - anything and everything they could reach through a telephone line and a modem. Like a twisted experiment gone awry, they escaped the carefully constructed confines of college labs and evolved. Another type of hacker had been born: the malicious hacker.

Computers and their related databases were so new at the time that no one had taken into consideration such things as questions of privacy. Computer intrusion wasn't yet a concern, because you had to know your stuff in order to even use a computer. Frankly, there weren't that many folks out there who did. But those who could invade the virtual world of others and take information which didn't belong to them didn't really care whose machine that information resided on or who the machine belonged to; whether a university, business, scientific institution or the federal government. If a hacker could get to the information, he could take it for his own use. That was just a fortunate byproduct of being computer literate, part of the elite group that could twiddle computers every which way. And twiddle they did!

Many hackers worked alone, riveted in front of desktop computers, tapping at their keyboards far into the night, using brute force and infinite patience to hack systems. Others joined with their peers, formed friendships and exchanged technical information about the latest systems and shortcuts. These informal groups could disseminate knowledge faster than any known conveyance.

Using computer bulletin boards, they left messages listing telephone numbers which had computers at the other end, they told each other what passwords to use to unlock the mysteries of unknown mainframes, they bragged about what systems they had hacked and how they had done it. Most of all, they formed a network of hackers who were convinced that there were no rules - at least no "real-world" rules - that applied to them. They made up rules of their own as they went along; their own peculiar sort of policies for what they considered the best game in the world: hacking.

But hacking wasn't a game, at least not to non-hackers. In 1978, a bank in Los Angeles lost $10.2 million when a hacker, a contract programmer who worked from inside, slipped into the computer system and diverted funds. Neal Patrick and members of Milwaukee's "414 Gang" hacked the Sloan Kettering Cancer Institute's computers and deleted the records of patients and the research notes of scientists. Hacking began to cost business big money and cause serious damage.

The 1980's were known as the "Decade of the Hacker," when the practice of hacking moved beyond innocent research; it became a crime. To help law enforcement agencies counter it laws such as the Computer Fraud and Abuse Act of 1986 and the Computer Security Act of 1987 were passed. But the laws did little to deter the hackers and their exploits continued.

In 1992, the National Oceanic and Atmospheric Administration (NOAA) discovered that a hacker had entered their system through its modem pool and breached its network in search of a free door to the Internet. December, 1993 saw AT&T urging businesses to be on guard against a possible increased risk of toll-fraud attempts by hackers.

An intruder alert was issued on the Internet on February 4, 1994, in an attempt to safeguard users from data loss resulting from password theft. The passwords were obtained by hackers using Trojan Horse programs, sniffers and other monitoring software. In the same month, United Press International told the story of two bachelors who had rented a billboard hoping to find perfect mates, and who subsequently became victims of a hacker who changed their voice mail message. Instead of a message telling callers how to get in contact with the men, callers heard an X-rated message.

Athletes and their families at the 1994 Winter Olympic Games were put on alert when it was reported that ice skater Tonya Harding's computer code number had been obtained by journalists. In March, 1994, a teenage hacker in Brooklyn calling himself "Iceman" joined with some of his friends and invaded the Internet-connected computers of Brooklyn's Polytechnic University and New York University's Courant Institute. They set out to obtain passwords and eventually managed to steal 103 of them.

The brotherhood of the hacker exists today, in a form no one - surely not the first college hackers - could have dreamt of. Former Assistant United States Attorney Kent Walker said, "In one year alone the FBI and U.S. Secret Service logged over 2,500 complaints of break-ins and attempted break-ins into computer networks." Hackers are part of the growing digital underground, a diverse group, some of whom are harmless, some of whom are malicious. Regardless of whether they do damage or not, no one wants them in their system. Unfortunately, hacking systems is their specialty.

A hacker gains access to computers that don't belong to him in one of two ways: either he goes directly to the source and finds an unoccupied terminal to work on, or he chooses the much easier and safer way of accessing the company mainframe through his own computer, hooked to a telephone line via a modem.

A modem (short for modulator/demodulator) takes computer data, transfers it from digital signals into audio impulses and sends them down a telephone line to another modem which then reconstructs the impulses back into readable digital data. A computer is an isolated entity until it is connected to a telephone line via a modem; then it becomes a communications device with untold potential for invading other computers connected to telephone lines. Once a computer is hooked to a phone line anyone can instruct their computer to call in and connect.

Today's businesses, corporations and research organizations find that phone access to their computers is essential for allowing their employees and related personnel to do their work. Unfortunately, the same phone line which is so convenient for authorized users is also an open door into company computers for unauthorized users who have somehow obtained the telephone number.

Data lines - phone numbers that connect a caller to a computer instead of a human being - may be public or private. Numbers that are publicly accessible are, of course, the easiest for hackers to find. Private numbers, which are generally intended for use only by authorized personnel, are harder to discover; but not impossible.

There are several ways in which a hacker trolls for active data lines. The first is by using a demon dialer or war dialer. These are computer programs which dial hundreds or thousands of numbers, one after the other, until a connection to a computer is made. That number is usually logged as a "hit" and the program continues to dial in sequence, looking for other data lines. Demon dialers can be detected by the phone company due to the sheer amount of numbers being dialed from one phone, although hackers are adept at routing their calls through different switches to throw off phone company traces. Using such a program also requires time and patience. Hackers sometimes like to use more direct methods, such as trashing (also known as dumpster diving), to obtain active data line numbers.

They say that you can learn a lot about a person - or a company - by looking through their trash. For hackers, trash isn't junk; it can be a gold mine of information. Somewhere among the company logs, files, mail and related paperwork can often be found such shiny gems as data line numbers, passwords and computer system information. Some companies even throw out old backup tapes when they begin to show signs of failure. One person's junk can be a hacker's treasure. Trashing often requires the physical act of invading private property and therefore carries some risk, not the least of which is arrest for trespassing and/or theft. Because of this, some hackers prefer to use their social skills.

"Social engineering" is the fancy name hackers have given to the art of lying to get what they want. "With the right words you can weasel just about any amount of information out of anybody," said an anonymous hacker who responded to my request for information about social engineering methods. "For instance, if I need to find out the network number for XYZ Institute, I'll just call their public number listed in the phone book. Whoever answers gets my standard spiel: I'm a technician with a computer repair company (sometimes I'll give them a false name) and I'm working on their computer glitch. Most systems have glitches, so this isn't usually suspect. I've misplaced the network access number and would they give it to me again, please. You can also get passwords this way. If you sound like a professional and you speak matter of factly, most of the time you'll get what you ask for."

Of course, accessing computers isn't as easy as just uncovering the phone number and calling. A hacker can have your data line number, but that won't get him into the system. Almost all computer systems and networks require that you have a valid account before you are allowed to use the system. System Operators or Administrators (sysops or sysadmins) who run individual computer networks are the cybergods who grant access to authorized users.

Say, for instance, that you are Joe Schmoe, an employee of a company we'll make up called Mach Aerospace. Part of your job involves traveling to various cities to offer technical support for your company's products. While away from the home office, you often need access to company information - technical diagrams, pricing, ordering information, manuals, etc. So your boss at Mach Aerospace gives you a telephone number. "Use a computer and a modem to call this number anytime you need access to company databases," she says. Along with the number she hands you a slip of paper with an account name and a password on it. These have been assigned to you by the sysop for your personal and exclusive use. Now, anytime you must connect with the company computer, all you need to do is dial up and enter your account name and password.

One of the sysop's responsibilities is to set your account up to grant you access to the information you may need; nothing more and nothing less. The sysop, of course, holds all the cards and all the power on the system. His account is high level and allows him access to all possible privileges. You, on the other hand, are just a user and so you have a low level account. Your account name and password allow you to operate only on a lower tier of access.

For a hacker, the account name and password are like Ali Baba's magical incantation "open sesame" - they are the keys to the cave. Getting the keys, however, is quite a bit more difficult than getting the telephone access number. Trashing may work, and so may variations on social engineering, but getting account names and passwords requires that a hacker use a good amount of guesswork and diligence.

Hackers are fascinated by computer systems and probably know more about any given system than the company or organization using it. If you spend any amount of time lurking on a hacker bulletin board, you will quickly realize that some of the most viable currency of the underground is information on computer operating systems and their security architecture. Once a hacker determines what type of operating system a computer is running, he knows how to plan his attack. His goal is to gain access to the highest level account he can attain.

Every operating system has a series of defaults; commands which were pre-set by the programmers before the system was shipped to the user. These defaults are often mundane. For instance, the system may use default colors of blue for the background screen and black for the on-screen text. A user can change this to a red screen with yellow text or any other desired combination. There are other defaults as well, and some of them aren't as mundane as your choice of screen colors.

Often, operating system defaults include an account name and password which allow access to maintenance accounts for system "housekeeping" or repair. These defaults are supposedly known only to the original programmers and the sysop currently in charge of the computer. Once distribution starts, however, these defaults quickly become common knowledge.

It has long been known, for instance, that the UNIX operating system has account name defaults of root, admin, sysadmin, unix, uucp, rje, guest, demo, daemon and sysbin. These accounts often do not have a password, and those that do sometimes use an identical password (username root has root as the password). It's up to the sysop to change these defaults as soon as the operating system has been installed and before users are allowed on. Unfortunately (fortunately, if you're a hacker!), many sysops just never get around to making the changes and the defaults stay in place; secret doors into the system.

If defaults don't get a hacker in, he moves on to Plan B. This may be where the hacker drives down to the company in the dead of night, parks behind the building and searches the trash bins, hoping to dig up an account name and password. As farfetched as it may sound, users are notorious for jotting this vital information down on just about anything handy - and then tossing it away. Again, trashing can be an informational gold mine for a hacker who has the nerve to take the chance.

Plan B may also consist of a hefty dose of social engineering. Hacker Bill Landreth, in his book *Out of the Inner Circle*, describes how he helped several hackers crack the account name/ password combination on an IBM-370 mainframe. "One of the hackers lived near the company, so I suggested that he write and print a one-page questionnaire on a letter-quality printer. He was to stand in the lobby and hand out about 150 copies to employees. He was to look and act student-like, and represent the questionnaire as a class project." The list asked for things such as name, address, title, job description, etc. It was a bold case of social engineering, and it worked. With this information, the hackers gained untold possibilities to work with in trying to figure out account names and passwords.

Beyond the triumvirate of defaults, trashing and social doubletalk there lies the most basic of the hacker's tools: simple guesswork. This is often the only way a hacker can force his way in. Account names are not secret and are often nothing more complicated than the user's first and last name. Depending on the system, there could be variations that use first name only, or last name only. Regardless, a hacker only has to acquire the names of several users and try them with different passwords. The password is the biggest secret, the nut which must be cracked.

Hackers say that there are two kinds of passwords: the outrageously easy to guess and the fiendishly difficult. Computer users generally don't put much thought into their password, preferring instead to use the easiest combination they can remember, such as their initials, birthdate or social security number. They are also fond of one word passwords such as "Computer," "Love," "Sex," "Open," and believe it or not, "Password."

Hackers sometimes run a dictionary program that tries to crack passwords by using common words taken from an online dictionary list. It is a slow, tiresome, boring process and using it often alerts sysops to the attempted intrusion, which means random password generators are not the best hacker tool.

A true hacker shouldn't have to use brute force to gain access, he should be able to use his knowledge of the system to exploit defaults or trap doors - "holes" in the system used by programmers for maintenance purposes. In his book *Information Warfare: Chaos On The Electronic Superhighway*, Winn Schwartau details several weaknesses a hacker can use to gain access to passwords, including the user himself, the memory inside the keyboard, the terminal emulator, the LAN (Local Area Network) connection card, the network cabling, the network server, other user nodes, the gateway, router, or bridge to other networks and the WAN (Wide Area Network) interface. You could say that a true hacker uses his brain and not his keyboard brawn to make his way in.

Hackers are notorious for wanting more power, more privileges on a system, and this is where hacking is most common: among legitimate users. A hacker who has a low-level account on a system usually wants a higher level account. Using finesse and a generous dollop of his programming skills, he can get it. The most frequent method of gaining higher access is called the Decoy. This method is a visual trick played on users, a program that a hacker writes to obtain account names and passwords. The Decoy program, when set loose by a hacker, clears the opening screen on a dial-in system and replaces it with a "phantom screen." The text looks just like the actual system screen, right down to the prompt for account name and password. The only difference is that when a user enters the account name/password combination the information is recorded and stored in a file to which the hacker has access. The Decoy program then tells the user that his entry attempt has failed and usually kicks him off the system or clears the screen and returns control to the real system. The user is then prompted to reenter his account name/password and all is once again normal; the user gains access on the second try and believes that the original failed log-on was simply a typing error or "computer glitch." After a few hours - or days - of this, the hacker has a file full of account names and passwords. One of them is bound to belong to a high level account.

An even bolder version of the Decoy involves setting up call-forwarding so that any call into the system computer is re-routed to the hacker's own computer. A false screen emulating the real system screen asks for the account name and password, tells the user it is incorrect and hangs up. Usually the line is kept open for a few minutes, forcing a busy signal on the user's next attempt at calling and re-routing the call to the real computer. This form of the Decoy method requires a personal contact within the telephone company (which many hackers are said to have) in order to get call forwarding set up on the company line.

A hacker with a low level account and the gift of gab may be able to do some online social engineering. Most systems have a chat feature which allows users to communicate with each other in real-time on the screen. A hacker can employ this feature to communicate with another user, perhaps convincing him that he is the sysop and needs to verify his password.

"One thing I used to good effect," an anonymous hacker told me, "was a sort of reverse suspicion thing. I would enter chat mode with a user, tell him that I was the sysop and that I was checking certain accounts for possible hacker activity. I put him instantly on the defensive by challenging his identity. Once you've got someone on the defensive, he isn't going to be questioning you, he's going to be trying to make you believe him. Most users will give you any information you want just to get out of the cold light of suspicion."

All of the tricks and shadowy moves we have talked about are methods that hackers use to enter a computer system from the outside. But the most insidious and far more common form of hacking comes from within, from employees or network users using their legitimate system access for unauthorized or illegal purposes.

HACKING FROM WITHIN

Organizations, companies, universities and online networks take the outside hacker threat seriously, much moreso than the threat of mischief from within their own ranks. The United States Department of Justice Computer Crime Unit has identified three reasons why this is so: first, the hacker threat is more recently encountered, while employee or "internal" theft has been around for quite awhile and is something that all companies are aware of and must deal with. Secondly, organizations usually do not know the purposes of hacker attacks, making those attacks appear to have no limitations. Third, hackers make organizations feel quite vulnerable because the hackers appear to be faceless, traceless attackers. The enemy who is perceived to be outside the walls, hiding in the shadows, always generates more fear than the enemy within.

Internal hacking, however, is far more prevalent than external attacks. It's the employee or user with rightful access to the organization's computer network that may well cause the most grief. According to a paper written by Michel Kabay of the National Computer Security Association (NCSA): "Information security specialists informally estimate that 80-85 percent of all computer crime is carried out by employees of the victimized firm."

In 1995, a study of 200 businesses conducted by David Carter, criminal justice professor at Michigan State University, revealed that 93.6 percent of the reporting businesses had been victims of computer crime and 43.3 percent of these had been computer crime victims at least twenty-five times. The study also found significant increases in the introduction of computer viruses into company machines and the harassment of employees through electronic mail and other network communications.

Carter said that research shows "the average business fraud is $23,000 while the average business fraud involving computers is $500,000." The most common computer-related abuses reported in the study were: credit card fraud 96.6 percent, telecommunications fraud 96.6 percent, employee use of company computer equipment for personal reasons 96 percent, unauthorized access to computer files for snooping 95.1 percent, cellular phone fraud 94.5 percent, unlawful copying of copyrighted or licensed software 91.2 percent. Theft or attempted theft of client or customer information was up 81 percent over the past five years, theft or attempted theft of trade secrets rose 77.6 percent, theft or attempted theft of new product plans reached 76.7 percent, unauthorized computer access to confidential employee information was up 74.5 percent, as was unauthorized computer access to confidential business information (74.4 percent) and theft or attempted theft of money at 72.2 percent.

Earlier we created a fictional character, Joe Schmoe of Mach Aerospace, to demonstrate how an employee of a company might require certain computer system privileges in order to do his job. Let's call on Joe again, this time to show how a little legitimate access can go a long way in the right hands.

Joe is an authorized employee, an avionics technician with the company. He has a valid mid-level account on the Mach Aerospace computer network, complete with password. Getting in is no problem; he does it nearly every day as part of his job. It's what he does while he's online that may create a problem. Since Joe is on the road most of the time, he is responsible for calculating his hours and especially any overtime worked. He has access to the Mach Aerospace payroll database, where he logs in this information. Joe has been with the company for several years; he's a good employee and is trusted to enter the correct information. But sometimes Joe adds an hour or two, padding his total. Mach Aerospace is a big company, he rationalizes. What's a few extra hours going to matter?

Joe's addition of a few hours to his overtime log constitutes data entry fraud. Anyone within an organization who deals with entering data into computers is capable of perpetrating this type of crime. It's dirt-simple for someone in the right position to change a "2" to a "4," remove an unauthorized long-distance phone call from a telephone log, or rearrange deposits so they are credited to another account.

All of these small but profound changes are known as "data diddling." Our buddy Joe isn't the only one who can engage in it: other users, data entry clerks, system operators and network programmers all have the basic expertise and opportunity to alter numbers. Some have the expertise to do much more and to cause damage as well.

"Software attack, often best carried out with the aid of well-placed insiders, is emerging as a coherent new type of systematic offensive warfare," wrote Yale University sociology professor Scott A. Borman, and mathematician Paul R. Levitt in the magazine *Signal*.

System programmers and other company insiders with the ability to manipulate operating systems have been known to create Logic Bombs, bits of computer code within the main program that are set to run only when a certain set of circumstances occurs. For instance, the bomb may be set to erase all files if the programmers' name is ever removed from the database or deleted from payroll records. Or it may be set to wait a specific amount of time before activating - days, months, even years. The Logic Bomb is a favorite of employees who are hedging their bets against the day they are fired or transferred.

Worm programs do even more treacherous (and virtually untraceable) work, such as transferring a minute amount of money on the first of the month from everyone's account into the programmer's own account (called the "Salami Technique"). Or they can be programmed to alter or destroy data, "crawling" through the operating system and wreaking havoc. All at the programmer's whim.

Employees with pure embezzlement on their minds like to use "Trojan Horses" to instigate the Salami Technique, slicing small amounts of money from hundreds of accounts. Trojans are also used to do hidden operations, such as capturing passwords.

It's also extremely easy for shrewd system operators to create back doors in the operating system to allow them access. The NCSA's Michel Kabay explains: "A trap door or back door is a testing aid left in programs to bypass normal security and program controls. For example, a programmer once told me of a program to calculate optimum file block size at his former employer's, which had an invisible terminal-read seven seconds after program initiation. If one knew which password to give - and when - one would be granted special undocumented capabilities which broke security restrictions."

The hacker with legitimate system access can cause no end of problems, some of them unseen and unknown until it's too late. For instance, it's not uncommon for computer users to keep important information on their hard disks: bank account numbers, tax information, resumes, personal letters and notes. Using a special program, a hacker can download these files from your computer while you are connected to an online service or network. And you'll never even know it's happening. "It's theft," said John Haggard, president of VASCO Data Security. "It's exactly the same thing as someone breaking into your home or automobile, except you lock your home and car."

Sniffers, also known as network analyzers, are meant to diagnose trouble on the network or to find vulnerabilities for system administrators. A hacker using one, however, can tell who is connected to the network, the amount of traffic passing over the net, where vulnerabilities exist, and even discover passwords and access codes. SATAN is an example of a network analyzer that has computer security experts worried; some have even gone so far as to call it an automated, point and click hacking tool. SATAN is a testing and reporting program that collects a variety of information about networked hosts and reports it back to the system running the program. SATAN finds vulnerabilities, places where hackers can attack to gain access. It was originally designed for system administrators, but hackers can get their hands on it too.

Whether the hacker is within or without, he can be a devastating presence, tying up mainframe time, corrupting programs, destroying, changing or stealing data and generally causing headaches. However, no matter who the hacker is or what type of access he has, he possesses one big gun that he can pull out and use anytime he wishes to go beyond mischief or theft and inflict wholesale destruction: the computer virus.

How to Protect Yourself from Computer Criminals

Cyber-Sneezes: Viruses

*"Even if no new viruses are created, there are already
enough circulating to cause a growing problem as they
reproduce. A major disaster seems inevitable."*
- John McAfee,
Computer Virus Industry Association.

Computer viruses originally began not as malicious programs
for hackers, but as intellectual games among researchers at
the Massachusetts Institute of Technology, AT&T Bell Laboratories
and Xerox Corporation's Palo Alto, Research Center. During their
off hours, programmers and researchers amused themselves and
their colleagues by diving into the core memories of company
machines. By altering the coding in those memories, they discovered that programs designed to digest data could also consume
data! This set off the infamous "Core Wars" game in which programmers matched wits against each other by devising programs
which had the ability to self-replicate and then consume the
programs of opposing players.

The viruses which were created during Core Wars were not
allowed to escape the confines of the research machines and so
they posed no real threat, at least to the outside world. The programmers, of course, kept the details of these viruses to themselves, so as to prevent malicious usage.

In 1983, Unix operating system creator Ken Thompson talked
about the Core Wars in a speech he made to the Association for
Computing Machines. That was a mistake. The following year

Scientific American magazine published an article about viruses, including an offer of detailed information on how to write such self-replicating programs. It wasn't very long before viruses had done a lot more than escape from the labs; they had begun to proliferate.

At first they were harmless programs, perhaps displaying a message on the screen or playing a tune at a certain time each day. Harmless, but annoying. But, like the hackers who started out innocently and soon turned to malicious acts, virus writers realized the power they held and began to create viruses that were more than simple annoyances; they were downright destructive.

Perhaps the most famous virus-related program was written and set loose in 1988 by Cornell University graduate student Robert T. Morris. It was called the Internet Worm because Morris set up his cyber-sneeze to spray at the world's first major computer network, the Internet. His worm brought the net to a virtual standstill by exploiting a flaw in the Sendmail program and reproducing itself endlessly. The reproductions took up large portions of processing and memory space, overtaxing computers and forcing shutdowns. It was a frightening demonstration of a new type of hacker tool, one that was quiet but deadly. And growing.

Working from what he says is the most conservative interpretation possible, Dr. Peter S. Tippett, Director of Security Products for Symantec Corporation, told a 1993 Congressional subcommittee of a report from IBM and DataQuest which "suggests that a company of only a thousand computers has a virus incident every quarter, that a typical Fortune 500 company deals with viruses every month, that the cost to a company with only a thousand computers is about $170,000 a year right now and a quarter of a million dollars next year. If we add these costs up, we know that the cost to United States citizens of computer viruses just so far, just since 1990, exceeds $1 billion."

THE COMMON COLD: TYPES OF VIRUSES

A virus is a computer program designed to infect other programs with copies of itself. Because it has the ability to reproduce it can spread from system to system, performing the mission its creator designed it for: damaging systems, deleting files, erasing hard disks. "Virus authors don't believe they are doing anything wrong, they don't believe that they are being harmful, and they don't believe that what they do is dangerous, but, in fact, all viruses are," said Symantec's Peter Tippett.

Most viruses attack software, often targeting the computer's operating system. Due to the various forms even one virus may take as a result of hacker manipulation, it is almost impossible to describe every virus known. John McAfee of the Computer Virus Industry Association (CVIA) and author of the book *Computer Viruses* says that viruses are classified by the architecture affected, the degree of disruption they cause, and the area of the system where the virus resides.

The CVIA estimates through reported and recorded infections that 70 percent of all viruses affect IBM PC's and related clones, while 24 percent affect the Apple and Amiga lines of personal computers. It is believed that the higher incidence of IBM infections is simply due to the greater popularity of this type of computer.

Most viruses are written to target a specific type of computer system and don't generally cross-infect other systems. The Internet worm that Robert Morris set loose, however, did infect both DEC Vax and Sun Microsystems computers, suggesting that perhaps viruses will cause wider damage in the future, as hackers become still more adept at writing them.

Viruses are often identified by the degree of disruption they cause to a computer system. Innocuous viruses are basically harmless and cause no noticeable problems with the system. They hide and quietly infect floppy disks and programs on the computer, all without damaging the host system. Joke or humorous viruses are invented, written and set loose purely for fun and cause no damage to the infected system; all they do is display a message or graphic and then disappear. They are annoying, but not particularly harmful, unless you count the system downtime needed to find and eradicate the virus, and the loss of productivity that sometimes occurs.

Altering viruses, on the other hand, are malicious. They search for and target system data. Once they find what they're looking for, these viruses change operating codes, transpose numbers and lines of code, remove digits and cause changes that are difficult to find. Catastrophic or destructive viruses are the most dangerous, simply because they are designed to cause wholesale destruction. They erase hard drives, programs or data, scramble the operating system and often crash the system.

Like a human virus that sets up housekeeping in your tonsils or lungs, computer viruses have favorite places they like to hide. The boot sector is the most common because it is the place which is accessed each time a computer is turned on. Think of the boot sector as the gatekeeper of the system, directing the computer to check here and there and do this and that at power-up before presenting the user prompt. Boot sector viruses are some of the most difficult to purge.

The second favorite area of infection is the operating system, which is the brain that runs the whole show, and may be considered the most important piece of software installed in the computer. Very few everyday computer users are familiar with the programming code of an operating system. This ignorance allows a virus writer to slip in a few lines of code which wouldn't be noticed by anyone but an experienced programmer.

Application programs are the third area of common infection. Applications are installed software that allow the computer to perform a task: word processing, spreadsheets, games, graphics, communications, etc. Viruses which use applications programs as their carriers like to lurk within the executable code, waiting for the program to be executed, at which time the virus is activated.

AH-CHOO! CATCHING A VIRUS

Human viruses and computer viruses part ways when it comes to their method of infection. Human viruses are able to pass from one person to another in a variety of ways; germs left on a doorknob, shaking an infected person's hand or simply by traveling through the air, borne on the wings of tiny droplets launched by a sneeze or a cough. Computer viruses, on the other hand, require direct contact before infecting. The virus must be introduced into the system, it cannot be caught through the usual human means.

Computer infection occurs primarily in two ways: a floppy disk unknowingly contaminated with a virus may be loaded into the system, setting the virus free from its diskette cage to romp through the larger confines of a computer, or a virus residing on a program or file on one computer may be transferred to another computer through communications lines, such as a bulletin board system (BBS) or network. Either way, the virus spreads.

Once a virus finds a path to a new home, it begins to stretch its legs, meander around, and sniff for receptive hosts which it can infect. The virus creator has given it certain targets; application programs or operating codes such as MS-DOS. Once it finds these recipients, it replicates and infects them. Anytime these new hosts contact another program, the virus will probe to see if it can infect further. If so, it replicates again and still another medium is contaminated. This contamination can go on indefinitely, depending on the virus writer's intentions. Unfortunately, there are many viruses with missions which go beyond repeated contamination; these types are programmed to alter or destroy.

A virus often activates after a specific number of infections occur, a certain amount of time has passed, or after a preset condition is met. The infamous Friday the 13th virus that first struck in 1989, came to life only on that date, lurking undetected until the calendar date triggered the internal program of the virus. The Michelangelo virus that frightened the computer community in March, 1992 operated in the same manner. Again, depending on the creator's intentions, a virus may activate immediately upon a new infection or it will wait. Usually it is instructed to wait a while and reproduce as much as possible, thereby spreading the infection far and wide. The virus writer's intention is to cause as much contamination as possible.

Once the infection phase of the virus is complete, activation occurs. Whatever the virus has been programmed to do, it now begins to do. Some activations are quite startling, such as a sudden deletion of all data, a system crash or a message on the screen, followed by the discovery that all system files have been erased. Other viruses are more subtle, eating away at data, changing a number here and there and slowly corrupting the system.

DAMAGE ASSESSMENT:
WHAT A VIRUS CAN DO

The first order of business for a virus is to reproduce at all costs. It may find twenty programs on your hard drive that are open to infection and it may create twenty copies of itself to attach to those programs. An inevitable side effect of this reproduction is that the replicated viruses occupy space on your computer, taking up precious memory that can't be used for anything else.

Viruses like to scramble files, rearrange the boot sector, change or delete data in programs and muddle the File Allocation Table (FAT) - the road map that describes where everything is on the hard disk.

Aside from altering data, viruses can be written which, when activated, will reformat your hard drive or the disks that are currently in your disk drives. They may totally reset your computer every time you attempt a power-up, or they may lock the keyboard so that the computer fails to respond to operator commands. Viruses can rewrite the keyboard recognition table so that your keystrokes don't do what they normally do, but perform other actions instead. Other viruses display harmless messages, tying up computer time, or cause programs to run at slower than normal speeds.

A variation on the standard virus is the Logic Bomb, mentioned earlier. Logic Bombs wait quietly until a certain set of conditions are met and then trigger, erasing files, reformatting your hard disk or causing other damage. Trojan Horses are similar to Logic Bombs. They take their name from the wooden horse used by the Greeks to enter and capture the city of Troy during the Trojan War. The computer version is a program that appears quite legitimate at first, perhaps even attractive, inviting the user to run it, while behind the scenes it is wreaking havoc. A popular Trojan Horse displays graphics on the screen to keep the user amused while it erases the hard disk.

THOSE NASTY BUGS

How do you know when your computer has contracted a virus? What do you do to rid your system of a virus? We will look at diagnosing and treating computer viruses and how to immunize your system against them in a later chapter. For now, it should suffice to say that the threat posed by hackers - both with their cunning when it comes to computer intrusion, and their ability to write destructive programs and set them loose - is very real. More real and more frightening, however, is the danger posed by criminals who use computers to directly attack our personal safety.

How to Protect Yourself from Computer Criminals

The Darkest Side of Computer Crime: Threats to Your Personal Safety and Property

> *"You can be fooled about people in cyberspace, behind the cloak of words...computer mediated communications provide new ways to fool people, and the most obvious identity swindles will die out only when enough people learn to use the medium critically."*
>
> - Howard Rheingold
> The Virtual Community

The computer criminals we have talked about so far have only one target: computers. Whether they are phone phreaks, hackers or virus writers, they all strive to explore, manipulate, and damage computers. Though the problems they cause may ultimately affect human beings at some level, it is usually financial or productivity losses that are incurred, not physical or mental harm.

"I don't care about the guy who owns the system, he's not my target; I care about the system itself and what's he got on it. I may leave a logic bomb, but that's only to destroy data on the computer. I may root around in his hard drive, but only to find and read information. That's what I'm interested in, the computer and what's on it, not the guy behind it," said a long-time hacker.

The impersonal computer with its associated hardware and software is the target of computer criminals. Personal harm toward people, either physical or mental, is usually not the aim. Unfortunately, there exists a class of computer criminal that is neither phone phreak, hacker, nor virus writer. He is much more. He is an online offender; a true criminal.

The online offender is usually not a hacker in the sense that we have come to know, but he may hack and he may use hacking methods in order to further the success of his crimes. However, he is usually not interested in the bits and bytes, the technical details of the way systems work and how deeply he can penetrate a system before being booted off. This type of criminal customarily has limited interest in hardware and software; the computer is simply a means to an end, it is not the end itself. The target of the online offender is people and he uses a computer with the intent of committing crimes against others, either directly through online contact or by information gained online. This puts him so far over the line into the criminal realm that to associate him with hackers is doing his victims a disservice, for he should be taken much more seriously than that.

CRIME ONLINE

It is easy to believe that the online world is different from the real world we live in. It's easy to think of the virtual world as a safe place because it exists behind a monitor screen, on the other side of the phosphor letters and at the end of a telephone line. Somehow the screen and the phone line are seen as barriers; they give us a a sense of invulnerability to harm. We cannot see the people who leave messages for us, the people that we respond to and chat with, and quite often we do not know them either. The computer allows a virtual fence to be erected between us and them, creating an illusion that we are protected. But these virtual fences can be climbed.

This place called cyberspace appears new, pristine, untouched and therefore safe; but it isn't. Detective Jim McMahon, a high-tech crimes investigator with the San Jose, California Police Department has tracked and apprehended criminals in cyberspace. "Everything that goes on in the real world happens there, too," he says. The parallel universe that is cyberspace may be invisible, it may have no physically definable dimensions, but it is not un-reachable, especially by those who would do harm.

You may participate in the online community for years and never run into an online criminal, and you may never be victim-ized by one who uses information obtained via computer to jeopardize your personal safety, privacy or property. There are no statistics on personal crime online and there are few verifiable cases. The known cases tend to be the boldest, the most outra-geous. We know that other cases exist, but their victims do not speak out and so we are left only with possibilities and probabili-ties. You may never encounter this type of computer crime, but as long as the possibility exists, forewarned is forearmed.

Personal crime online involves the personal contact crimes of impersonation, harassment, threatening messages, stalking, pedophiles and fraud. The online offenders who engage in these illegal activities do so while their computers are connected to other computers via a modem. They prowl those realms of cyberspace which can only be visited through the phone lines.

GUESS WHO?

Howard Rheingold, author of *The Virtual Community*, said it best when he wrote that "you can be fooled by people in cyberspace, behind the cloak of words." The online community lives and breathes through words, and users are simply names attached to messages. Exactly who is behind a name seen online is up for discussion.

Most commercial bulletin boards require that you use your real name, but you can never be one hundred percent sure that, say, "Mike Smith" is really Mike Smith; he may be anyone, he could even be a she. There are no guarantees that, just because the rule says real names must be used, that they are used. With the proliferation of free start-up kits for online services it's easy for a user to pick up several and possibly register each under a different name.

Various online services and BBSs allow users to change their names so that, for instance, Mary Jones can become virtually anyone she wants to be while in cyberspace. Her real identity is on the billing logs, but the name she uses as she browses the message topics may be different. Some bulletin board services even allow the use of pseudonyms - pen names that hide the real identity of the user. With pseudonyms, you don't know who you are really talking to. You may never know.

Computer users can't see each other, so relationships are built on trust. You simply have to take the other person at face value, believing that they are who they say they are. In most cases, they are legitimate. Mike is Mike and Mary is Mary and all is well in cyberspace. But the possibility of impersonation is still high. Gary Chapman, writing in the April 2,1995 edition of *The New Republic* magazine said, "Network users lie, sometimes spectacularly."

Someone, somewhere, may decide to use the cloak of words to hide their identity. The cloak is virtually impenetrable by the average person and thus it gives a feeling of safety to those who choose to misrepresent themselves. It emboldens them to do and say things they normally wouldn't. The cloak of words may become a license to deceive.

Deception takes several forms, most notably that of identity. It starts with using a different name, but it can extend farther than that. You may choose to tell others you meet online that you are a brain surgeon, when in fact you flip hamburgers for a living. Or you can say that you look like California's entry in the Miss America contest when the truth is closer to Ma Kettle's daughter. Unless you get specific and give out too many details which can be checked, you will probably be believed. Women have been known to pose as men to avoid sexually suggestive messages and e-mail, and men have been known to pose as women.

Author Jill Smolowe, in her article "Intimate Strangers" (*Time* magazine special issue, Spring, 1995) said that "the disembodied voices that whisper through cyberspace can often be manufactured identities that can disguise, distort or amplify aspects of a user's personality." This, for the most part, is relatively harmless. *Love Over the Wires* author Paulina Borsook calls this type of misrepresentation "selective lying by omission." But there are those who take it to a level beyond little white lies, beyond the mostly harmless.

Because anyone can represent himself as almost anybody, even a famous person, and with the right details, pull it off, you can never be quite sure who's on the other end of the line. Alan Blatecky, Vice President of Information Technologies at MCNC, a research consortium based in North Carolina, says that in the real world it's easy to identify people via sounds and visual clues, but on a computer "how do I know it's you?"

A well-known true crime author related a puzzling impersonation episode that happened to him. It seems he was being impersonated on a commercial online service that he didn't even have an account with. The impersonator used information he got from the author's books to make him sound legitimate. Under this guise, the impersonator fooled others into thinking that he was actually the author. Apparently he was rather rude to several of the author's fans while online. As you can imagine, this type of thing can impact a person's career and overall credibility.

Fortunately, the number of users who misrepresent themselves online is relatively small. Though misrepresentation may prove hurtful to those who have been fooled, there are more malicious activities that far overshadow this practice.

FOOTSTEPS AMONG THE BYTES: HARASSMENT AND STALKING ONLINE

"Jane" is an advertising executive who uses a personal computer at home to work on projects. In what little spare time she has available she enjoys participating in a popular online information service. Sometimes she uses it for information retrieval related to her job and sometimes she uses it for the fun of talking to others interested in the same topics she is.

Just three months after she began exploring the message boards, leaving her thoughts and comments, she became the victim of an online stalker.

"At first, all he did was leave cute little messages on the same topic areas that I was on. Then he started bashing my opinions and generally trying to make everyone believe that I didn't know what I was talking about. He would take the least little thing I said and twist it around so it came off meaning something else," Jane said. "After a week or two of this, I stopped posting on my favorite section and went to another. Well, he found me there and started all over again. When I publicly told him to stop following me around the service, he began sending me nasty e-mail messages threatening me. Since the messages were private, only I knew what was happening. It was out of the public eye now. I reported it to the administration of the service, but got nowhere. He changed his name and kept it up. Pretty soon I was tired of it and canceled my membership. I use a local bulletin board system now, and I haven't seen him there yet."

Jane's experience is typical cyber-bullying, a vicious kind of game that some play in varying degrees online. It has several levels, beginning with "flaming," a quite legal frontal assault conducted by an individual who disagrees with or misinterprets something you've said and decides to start an argument with you. "Electronic conversations appear to be prone to misinterpretation, sudden and rapidly escalating hostility between the participants...," Gary Chapman wrote in *The New Republic* magazine.

Flaming is allowed on most bulletin boards, though it is usually monitored by moderators and sysops to see that it doesn't get out of hand. As long as the message is attacked, and not the messenger, things are usually allowed to proceed without any intervention. Flame messages can go back and forth for months, as long as both sides continue to stoke the fires. It's only when flaming degenerates into nasty personal attacks that the messages get clipped on services such as CompuServe, Prodigy or America Online. Private bulletin boards and the Internet have been known to let flame wars continue without injecting any type of control.

Flame wars can get profane and hateful, but when one side backs off the fire often dies down and sputters out. The control is solidly in the hands of the those directly involved, and who are mostly willing participants at that. When one side becomes unwilling to continue, the other flamer has to look for someone else to argue with. Flame wars are relatively harmless and lend the online world some of its free-spiritedness. However there are other levels beyond mere flaming that cross the line from innocent to malicious.

The harassment that Jane described earlier is sometimes unprovoked; it may come from someone you have never encountered online before or it may come from someone who has taken a dislike to you and your views. Often it originates with someone who is bored and thinks it's fun, a way of getting "kicks." Any way you look at it, this cannot be construed as flaming; this is outright harassment. It doesn't stop when you ask it to and it doesn't stop when you reply with snappy comebacks. It just doesn't stop. That's harassment, and most online services and many system operators will terminate a person's account if they engage in too much of it.

Harassment takes many forms online, the most common being content-related. Messages may be directed to you that are nasty or downright mean, profane, sexually suggestive or derogatory. A reporter for *Computer Life* magazine once posed on the Internet as a 15-year-old cheerleader and got more than 30 e-mail messages of a sexual nature. Harassing messages are often public, depending on the service on which they are posted, and can even be libelous. You can't fight a lie and harassing messages have thrown doubt on more than one person's credentials and views. In public this can be hurtful, in private it can be frustrating.

Those who send harassing messages occasionally like to flood a victim's electronic mailbox with them. This sometimes has the effect, once the mailbox has hit its memory limit, of preventing legitimate messages from being delivered.

A favorite of harassers is the electronic mail bomb, collections of messages designed to shock, annoy and disturb those who get them. Sometimes a mail bomb is disguised as legitimate mail, but once opened it reveals distasteful and often pornographic materials. Mail bombs have also been set loose into Internet message bases, which totally ruins everyone's day and drives system operators crazy. These public bombs are not directed at anyone personally, but they can be considered harassment on a much larger scale because they affect thousands of users.

Another popular form of online harassment occurs when a user is followed by a harasser to different message bases and topics. One user related his story of being followed by a female harasser who showed up in all the areas where he posted. She would respond to any message he wrote to anyone, and her replies were often negative and belittling. "She never directly threatened me, but she always put down what I said, whether she knew what I was talking about or not. It become completely annoying after awhile; it was like I couldn't go anywhere without her being there, watching and listening."

Sometimes the message content from a harasser takes a turn toward the dark side and may become truly frightening. When the messages become personally threatening rather than only disparaging, they become something beyond mere harassment: online stalking.

The online stalker is much like the real world stalker; his goal is often intimidation and the engendering of fear in the person he pursues. Though the stalker is often male, females have also been known to engage in the practice. Online stalking usually begins with a period of testing, during which the stalker attempts to provoke a response. This response may be a public or private reply asking him to cease and desist, or it may take the form of public messages to others about the stalker's activities. Either way, a response is what the stalker is seeking; something that indicates his overtures are striking home. Once he provokes this response, he begins to escalate the testing of his target.

The testing escalation can take the form of an invasion of an online user's "personal space" - the message bases he or she frequents - through incessant posting and following a user from area to area. The testing customarily takes the form of harassment, making it difficult to determine if you simply have a harasser on your hands, or a true stalker. The break point comes when the stalker moves out of the testing phase and into threats and intimidation, either by public messages or more commonly by private e-mail.

Beth Givens at the Privacy Rights Clearinghouse tells of a call received there from a woman who was being stalked via e-mail at her job. "The stalker worked on the same campus and also made his presence known in the building in which she worked. Because of the persistence of the messages and the threats they contained, she left her job and moved to another city."

Most computer users who engage in online communications can deal with stalkers who simply follow them around electronically.

They can even deal with the threats and intimidation, usually by ignoring them or reporting them to system administrators. Online stalking can be annoying, irritating, unnerving and exasperating, but it is not usually harmful.

The real problem occurs when the stalker takes his stalking beyond the electronic realm. Using hacking techniques or browsing through publicly available databases, the stalker begins to gather information on his target. The sheer amount of personal information about anyone that can be found through computer databases is shocking. To begin with, your name, address and telephone number may be contained on a disk; a CD-ROM called *Phone*File*. Several companies market similar directories and you can buy the latest copy at the local software store. The online service you subscribe to may also have a nationwide phone directory available for your use; just pay a connect-time fee and run your search. Any public library that has entered the information age will also have this type of database. Enter a name and up comes all the matches from across the country, including address and telephone number. Anyone can access this information about you.

Using public databases to dredge up information on his target, the stalker may begin to send messages in which he tells the target what he knows: the target's address, telephone number, social security number, voting record, the kind of vehicle he or she drives, income - the list goes on and on. This, coupled with the threats, are enough to scare anyone. The online stalker occasionally steps way over the line and actually begins stalking in the traditional way: calling the target on the telephone, leaving threatening or suggestive messages on an answering machine, sending letters or packages through the mail and maybe, if he's close enough geographically, following the target around in the "real world."

A 1995 *Newsweek* Poll found that 80 percent of those asked were concerned about being harassed by virtual stalking through unwanted messages and 76 percent were concerned about being harassed by real stalking from someone they first met online. That fear is not altogether unfounded. The *New York Times* reported in September, 1994 that an Internet user was to stand trial in Michigan for harassing a woman with e-mail messages and by leaving messages on her telephone answering machine. Andrew Archambeau admitted to courting a woman he met through a dating service, but said that he intended her no harm. Archambeau sent about twenty e-mail messages, as well as letters and packages through the regular mail.

All fifty states maintain stalking laws, but electronic stalking is not as widely addressed. In 1995, Connecticut became one of the first states to enact a law making harassment by computer a crime. As this is written electronic stalking legislation is finally being considered by both houses of Congress.

Online stalking may never move beyond the electronic confines of a computer, but whether it does or not, it is a very real and potentially dangerous practice that must be recognized and dealt with.

Adults are commonly the targets in computer stalking cases, but children have been crime victims, too. When it comes to victimizing children online, the worst kind of criminal leads the list: the computer pedophile.

WHAT'S YOUR NAME?
COMPUTER PEDOPHILES AND PORNOGRAPHY

Children are trusting individuals who have a natural curiosity and a zeal for exploring the world around them. These attributes are prized and even cultivated by parents. They are the qualities we all wish we could recapture in our own lives. As adults, we have come to learn that not everyone is worthy of trust and what we have learned as a result of our curiosity has sometimes been hurtful. Many of us are therefore cautious of our outside contacts to a certain extent and we try to protect ourselves. Most children, however, have not yet learned this lesson and so they are open to harm. In the real world we can work to protect them, but in the online world children may quickly become involved in activities and relationships that are less than desirable, simply because of the nature of the medium and the widespread exposure of children to computers.

"We face a unique, disturbing and urgent circumstance, because it is the children who are the computer experts in our nation's families," said Senator Dan Coats (R-Indiana).

There are few barriers in cyberspace and there are virtually no visual cues to help children put into practice all of the things they are commonly taught to protect themselves from strangers and from harm. Online, the very traits which make children such precious individuals can lead them into temptation and danger. It is not the children's fault that this can happen, it is primarily the fault of the child predators who use computer bulletin boards as their hunting ground.

"BBSs are the new playgrounds, and the number of kids online who fit a pedophile's victim profile is very high," said Alfred Olsen, a police chief in Pennsylvania who has assisted in over one hundred online pedophile investigations.

In 1994 a 24-year old Chelmsford, Massachusetts man, John Rex, Jr., was charged with using a BBS to induce a teenager to assist him in kidnapping a young boy. In 1995, 15-year old Daniel Montgomery met a new friend in a gay and lesbian chat room on America Online. Daniel and Damien Starr began exchanging e-mail. Not long after, Daniel received a bus ticket in the mail and left home. He was found waiting in a San Francisco airport terminal. Daniel told his parents that Damien was an older teenager and that he hadn't been harmed by him. Shortly after that story made news headlines, 13-year old Tara Noble of Kentucky was lured to California by a man she had met online.

In San Jose, California, Donnell Howard Hughes used a BBS to exchange pornographic discussions via e-mail with someone he believed to be a 13-year old boy. The discussions lasted two months before Hughes finally asked the boy to meet him face to face. The "boy" who arrived for the meeting turned out to be San Jose Police Detective Jim McMahon, who arrested the 51-year old insurance agent. "Once candy was the lure," wrote *Los Angeles Times* staff writer Kim Murphy. "Now strangers are using cyberspace e-mail to attract minors into harm's way."

While law enforcement experts say that pedophiles online are a very small fraction of the total number of computer users, their existence has been recognized and should be acknowledged.

A pedophile may be young or old and belong to any nationality or race, however, the one constant is that they are generally male. According to the American Psychiatric Association's Diagnostic and Statistical Manual of Mental Disorders (DSM-III-R), his age is arbitrarily set at "sixteen years or older and at least five years older than the child." He can be the guy living next door or the fellow standing beside you in the check-out line at the grocery store. In today's world he can also be someone faceless and unknown, a name at the other end of a computer message.

Computer pedophiles find victims in cyberspace in much the same way they do in the real world: they search for likely candidates. On bulletin board systems, likely candidates are found in places where children gather; places such as chat rooms, teen talk sections, and message bases devoted to music, television, movies, games, sports and automobiles.

"Some pedophiles," according to Supervisory Special Agent Kenneth V. Lanning of the Federal Bureau of Investigation Behavioral Science Unit, "can watch a group of children for a length of time and then select a potential target." In the online world this watching amounts to browsing the messages bases, reading the notes that children post to each other and getting to know a child through them.

The child the pedophile eventually selects has characteristics common to many children: natural curiosity, easily influenced by adults, a need for attention and affection and sometimes a need to defy their parents. Sometimes the child is from a broken home or is a victim of some type of neglect, either emotional or physical. These factors may make the child extremely susceptible to overtures from adults. The skill for finding this type of victim "is developed through practice and experience," says Agent Lanning.

Pedophiles know how to talk to children. They often have the same interests and hobbies and can easily engage a child in conversation about a favorite topic, creating a near-instant rapport. They know how to listen and pay attention to what a child believes is important. In fact, Lanning calls pedophiles "master seducers of children" because they identify with them so well.

Once an online pedophile finds a potential victim, he begins to seduce him or her by exchanging frequent messages and gradually gaining the child's confidence. The attention and affection the pedophile expresses often cements the friendship.

Once a camaraderie is developed, the pedophile begins to break down the child's inhibitions by discussing matters of a lewd or sexual nature. The messages may be quite explicit and may include fantasy writings or narrative descriptions. The pedophile may also send the child pornographic pictures in the form of digitized images known by acronyms such as GIF, JPG or BMP. The final goal of all of this is personal contact and it comes when the pedophile asks the child to meet him in person, in which case the computer becomes just a means to an end.

Law enforcement officials say that while pedophiles do use computers to support their schemes and occasionally to recruit victims, they are far more likely to use computers and modems to collect, trade and distribute child pornography and related information. Police investigations have uncovered computer files containing correspondence, photograph collections, names, addresses and even records of contacts with children. Agent Lanning, in his behavioral analysis of child molesters, writes that "the computer helps fill their needs for organization, validation and souvenir records."

Electronic mail, too, becomes another high-tech tool for pedophiles, who use it to talk with other pedophiles and exchange digital images, animated sequences, mailing lists and catalogs. The messages and photos are often encrypted so that they cannot be read or traced by anyone but the intended recipient.

In 1995, an issue of *Boardwatch* magazine stated that children have a far greater chance of being victimized by a pedophile in the non-computer world than they do online. Still, the threat is very much there. Several highly publicized cases of pedophiles using computers have caught the attention of the media and ten to twelve high profile child seductions were noted in 1994, but reported cases are relatively infrequent. It must be remembered, however, that crimes against children are usually hidden and often go unreported by victims because of intimidation, fear, or threats of being harmed.

Most bulletin board system and commercial online service operators watch for improper messages and advances, especially in the youth oriented sections. For the most part, sysops are quick to squelch anything that might look inappropriate. For this reason, it is more likely that children online will discover pornography than pedophiles in their daily surfing of the cyberwaves.

ONLINE PORNOGRAPHY

Pornography, also known by the legal term obscenity, is commonly described as any material, pictures, films, printed matter or devices dealing with sexual poses or acts considered indecent by the public. The first federal anti-pornography law was passed in the United States in 1842; the mailing of pornographic materials becoming illegal in 1865. Distributing and selling pornography is illegal in most countries, but what is considered pornography has been hotly debated through the years, making enforcement difficult at best.

The United States Supreme Court has attempted to define obscenity. The 1973 Miller versus California ruling resulted in a three-part definition of obscenity: matter that appeals to prurient interests, offends current standards, and has no redeeming social value. If the material meets all three standards, it is considered obscene and is not protected under the First Amendment of the Constitution.

The Court also amplified its earlier decision, ruling that states could decide on individual questions of obscenity by applying contemporary community standards to judge whether or not material is pornographic. As the Court said, "the people of Maine or Mississippi [should not be required to] accept the public depiction of conduct found tolerable in Las Vegas, or in New York City." The Miller test, as it has come to be named, can easily be applied to material found in cyberspace.

All of the commercial online services prohibit obscenity, though not all of them call it that in so many words. CompuServe, for instance, has this to say in their operating rules: "Member agrees not to publish on or over the Service any information, software or other content...which would be abusive, profane or offensive to an average person..." Anyone who signs up with this service must agree to the rules before being accepted.

CompuServe also says that "Member agrees not to use the facilities and capabilities of the Service to conduct any business or activity or solicit the performance of any activity which is prohibited by law..."

Most states have laws against the promotion - defined as the manufacturing, selling, transferring, distributing, mailing, giving away, lending, exhibiting or advertising - of obscene materials. These laws could be applied to cyberspace. Non-obscene materials that may be lawfully distributed are commonly restricted to adults only. When they are disseminated or shown to minors they may violate state laws.

Two federal laws apply: 18 USC Section 1465 prohibiting interstate transportation of obscene material for sale or distribution and 47 USC Section 223 prohibiting obscene communications through telephone lines. The first law may impact users who access obscene materials from BBSs located in other states, while the second may impact any obscene materials transmitted from one computer to another.

In 1982 the Court upheld a New York statute that prohibited the production and sale of materials depicting children in sexually explicit situations. This case placed child pornography in the speech category, and therefore not protected by the Constitution's First Amendment. Most states have child pornography laws that prohibit materials depicting minors (usually anyone under the age of eighteen) in a sexually explicit manner. Federal child protection laws make it a crime to create, possess or disseminate child pornography. In cyberspace, digital images and related animated sequences involving minors in sexual situations qualify as child pornography, while written materials may not qualify and must be examined under the Miller test.

18 USC Section 2252 bans child pornography and specifically forbids the use of computers to transmit such. It's considered a federal offense to upload or download child pornography.

In September, 1995, the FBI made at least a dozen arrests and searched 120 homes nationwide during the conclusion of a two-year investigation into the use of America On Line to distribute child pornography and arrange sex with children. It was the first time computer users were investigated by a federal agency for using a commercial network to exchange child pornography. "We are not going to permit exciting new technology to be misused to exploit and injure children," said Attorney General Janet Reno.

In 1995, the U.S. Senate added an amendment to a major telecommunications bill which provides federal penalties in cases where children are exposed to pornography through computer networks or when such materials are transmitted. It also puts the onus on computer services such as CompuServe and AOL to keep children away from indecency on their services. The true impact of this bill is yet to be known, as it is still undergoing challenges.

Generally, children are safe from encountering pornography in the public areas of commercial online services. E-mail on these same services, however, is another matter. Though rules like CompuServe's clearly prohibit the distribution of obscene materials through electronic mail, it is still possible to do so. It is alleged that some services may spot check or randomly read private mail and others periodically run e-mail messages through content-checkers programmed to look for certain words or phrases. The Prodigy online service controls public message content through an automatic software screening program and an emergency delete function. Encrypting e-mail can easily foil these attempts at enforcing obscenity rules. Most commercial services just rely on the user to follow the rules.

Private bulletin board systems are another matter entirely. Many of these BBSs have an adult section where pornography can be viewed online or downloaded. Access is routinely restricted and those users that request access may be voice-validated with a phone call from the sysop. They may also be required to submit a copy of their driver's license or other identification for age verification. Sysops don't need the headache of being caught and prosecuted for allowing minors to obtain pornographic materials.

Some bulletin boards, however, cater to those seeking pornography. Take for instance, this private BBS which advertised "Gigabytes of Sleeze, Erotic Stories, Games, and Graphic Pictures." The ad went on to say that "this adult BBS is not for the meek and mild. The system is a remote bulletin board for perverted owners of computer systems...we have thousands of programs, erotic stories, and pictures that can be obtained by calling with your computer and downloading. Now you don't have to wait for a brown wrapper mail order, you can get the programs instantly by computer." A *Time* magazine article reported that there are literally thousands of BBSs such as this one dealing in adult oriented materials. The five largest systems are said to have revenues that annually exceed one million dollars.

An extensive study of online pornography conducted by Pittsburgh's Carnegie Mellon University found that "trading sexually explicit imagery is one of the largest (if not the largest) recreational applications of users of computer networks." As an example, the study surveyed Internet Usenet newsgroups that handle digital images and found that 83.5 percent of the images were of a pornographic nature. The study is quick to point out, however, that pornographic images represent only three percent of all Usenet messages. The Carnegie Mellon report, entitled *Marketing Pornography on the Information Superhighway*, goes on to say that 98.9 percent of the users that access pornographic images online are men. This report has been widely criticized as inaccurate. Only when further studies are done will we be able to compare and come to our own decisions about how widespread pornography is online.

Much of the adult fare found on private BBSs are scanned images of magazine photos, no different from what you will find on a magazine stand at a bookstore or corner 7-11 store. Increasingly, however, the adult BBS market is being driven by images that you can't easily find: subjects such as pedophilia and hebephilia (youths). Those who collect such images prefer to keep their desires to themselves, and so anonymously viewing, downloading and storing these pictures on a personal computer can be extremely appealing.

Crime online doesn't always consist of a harasser or stalker's virtual footsteps following you, or a pedophile dogging your children; it may also be a much more common crime: fraud.

OLD CRIME, NEW TWIST: FRAUD

He had all the right answers and the enthusiasm to go with them. To hear him tell it - and tell it he did to anyone who would pay attention to his online ramblings - he was the owner and president of a software company and his programs were cutting-edge. "Hop on aboard and be a distributor and you'll be rich in no time," was the basic message; his actual wording was much more subtle. In no time he had takers, people willing to shell out their hard earned cash to become a part of the company. He took the cash and gave them very little in return. They didn't get rich because the product wasn't as cutting-edge or as lucrative as he claimed. They didn't make money, but he did. It was a classic case of fraud, perpetrated exclusively over a computer bulletin board. No one knew the fraudster's real name and he was virtually untraceable. There's no doubt that the online world offers definite benefits to the con artist.

Cyberspace is the perfect territory for running cons. Get rich quick scams and pyramid schemes usually require and thrive on a large number of people becoming involved. Gathering together such a group is often difficult because the public has been drilled to watch out for the more common scams.(See my book *The Ripoff Reader* from LimeLight Books.) The normal means of contacting and drawing people into a scam - U.S. mail, telephone, door to door - are well known and anticipated. Cyberspace, however, has several things going for it that the real world does not: millions of possible dupes, quick dissemination of information, and anonymity. A con artist looking for a new avenue need look no farther than the virtual world.

The Internet is the largest collection of interconnected computers, outdoing the commercial online services and private bulletin boards. A con artist looking for suckers has only to jump on the information superhighway. World usage of the Internet grew 95 percent in 1994 and twenty-two nations joined the net that year. At last count 159 nations were interconnected electronically. In the United States, 3.2 million computers are connected to the Internet and every thirty seconds, another network of computers joins the net worldwide. A *U.S. News and World Report* story in February, 1995 reported that, worldwide, there were 56,000 organizations interconnected, 32,000 businesses, 1.3 million business computers (up 628 percent in just three years!), 1.1 million school and university computers and 209,345 government computers. In May, 1996, a story in the same magazine reported that the number of Internet users worldwide was expected to hit 50 million by the end of that year. What more could a con artist want? As far as a cross-section of possible victims goes, the online world is more than adequate for a swindler's desires.

A message posted on the Internet has the ability to zip to computers around the world and back in a very short period of time. During its journey, the message can easily be read by millions of people. Anyone can choose to respond to this message, allowing a con artist's net to have an almost limitless reach.

In Salt Lake City in 1995, a 15-year old boy made $10,000 by posting an Internet ad selling bogus computer-related items. Buyers who sent money received an empty package sent COD or nothing at all. The boy was arrested for second-degree computer and credit card fraud and theft.

Trolling for dupes with a virtual net can be done anonymously. It's quite easy for anyone to simply use one of the many available anonymous remailers. Remailers are free e-mail forwarding sites that strip off the user identification and sometimes also the origination site from the header on electronic messages. After going through this filtering process, the mail is then sent on anonymously, making it nearly impossible to trace. A con artist can find plenty of places to hide in the relative anonymity of the computer world.

Conning someone, of course, doesn't have to occur on a grand scale. The swindler may choose just one target, someone online who perhaps has expressed a problem with finances or his job situation. The online society encourages the lessening of inhibitions, and people find themselves admitting things that a con artist can latch onto in order to work a scam. No matter if the scam is directed toward one person or ten thousand, in the end it can be just as harmful. "We're trying to tell people to be careful," said Denise Voigt Crawford, Texas Securities Commissioner, "there is a new fraud on the horizon."

Whether it's harassment, stalking, pedophiles, pornography or fraud, these crimes all have one basic feature: invasion of privacy.

TOO CLOSE FOR COMFORT: INVASION OF PRIVACY

The United States Constitution guarantees many things, but the right to privacy has never been specifically within its wording. Nevertheless, a person's privacy is generally upheld by the Third and Fourth Amendments to the Constitution which prohibit unlawful searches and seizures. Although these two amendments apply to protection from privacy invasions by the government, general privacy has been inferred from them. In fact, Justice William O. Douglas, in his decision in Griswold versus Connecticut, wrote that the "right to privacy is older than the Bill of Rights." Douglas reasoned that a person's privacy existed in the penumbra of the Third and Fourth Amendment guarantees.

We cannot fault the framers of the Constitution for not specifically mentioning privacy, because privacy as we know and wish for it today was not a large problem then. There were only a limited number of ways in which a person's privacy could be invaded, and most of them had to do with invasion of privacy by the forces of government. Those invasions were dealt with nicely by the Constitution, but defining any other forms of privacy has always been a problem.

In Olmstead versus United States, Justice Louis Brandeis called privacy the right to be let alone. Alan Westin, in his book *Privacy and Freedom*, wrote that he believed privacy should be defined as the right of persons to control the distribution of information about themselves. Westin's words perhaps come closest to touching on our current concerns about the subject. With the passage of time and the explosion of technology, personal privacy has become a question; it is no longer a given.

We can lock the doors and pull down the window shades in our homes against prying eyes, but when our personal information escapes the confines of our four walls and takes up residence in the databases and files of computer systems and networks, privacy becomes a rather tenuous thing. The National Institute of Standards and Technology's Computer Systems Laboratory states that "the accumulation of vast amounts of electronic information about individuals by the government, credit bureaus, and private companies combined with the ability of computers to monitor, process, aggregate, and record information about individuals have created a very real threat to individual privacy." Out there, drifting among the bits and bytes for almost anyone to access, is information about you, your home, your personal tastes and your past history.

"The amount of information I can get for an individual is enormous," said Allan Blatecky of research consortium MCNC. "I can look at where you call, where you buy. Put it all together and we are getting a far better description of you than you would imagine." And a far better description than you may care for anyone to have without your knowledge and express permission.

Dr. Peter Tippett, data security manager for a software company in Washington state, once came face to face with a database of information on himself that he had no idea existed. Searching Prentice-Hall Online, Tippett casually entered his own name and watched as records on his life scrolled past on the monitor screen. The information included the addresses of Tippett's previous residences, the cost of his current home, the number of bathrooms in it, the size of his front yard, median income for households in his census area and even a copy of his medical license. As Tippett discovered, online access to personal information about someone can be easy: "I can be standing behind an attractive woman in a grocery line, glance at the name on her check and find out later through a computer where she lives, her number and who she lives with."

What do you want to know? Somewhere a database exists with the information you seek and for a fee, or the price of a phone call, you may be able to tap into it. Take CompuTrace, for example, a feature of the CompuServe commercial online service. CompuTrace will give you the last known address of almost anyone: just enter a name and let the database do a search. Or how about Phone*File, available online or at many local libraries. I've searched this database, which is much more accurate than it's made out to be. Enter a name and up pops an address and phone number. Are you listed? Probably.

While the electronic frontier has opened up great new opportunities for us all, it has also allowed access to information that was never before available without showing up in person at some government office, hat in hand. If you were interested in the data listed on someone's voter registration card, you showed up between nine and five, asked politely and the clerk gave you what you wanted.

Today, you may be able to obtain the same information just by directing your modem to dial the right number. No one sees you, no one knows who you are. Public records are just that: public. If you know where to look there's very little you can't find out. And that is perhaps the most frightening part of the entire concept of privacy: our personal safety may be threatened.

What type of things can someone find out about you? Driver's license information, Department of Motor Vehicles records, results of civil and criminal court cases, credit history, information about household members, telephone numbers, addresses, where you work, how much you're paid, where you shop, what type of things you purchase, what clubs or associations you belong to, where you go on vacation and what time of the year you go, your medical condition, and marital status.

Granted, most of this is public information and you don't need a computer to access it. However, computers have made information retrieval considerably easier and have allowed many records to be compiled in databases. Richard H. Baker, author of the *Computer Security Handbook*, wrote: "automated systems reduce the cost and time barriers that previously tended to protect this information and provide wider access to public records."

Rusty Coats, a writer for the McClatchy News Service, says that the bits and bytes of information about you make up your digital shadow, which he calls a "mutation of electronic evolution." Coats wrote that computers have put information literally just a keystroke away, and that everyone's life has been recreated digitally in database files. These files are sold to information brokers and businesses and "the big loser in the trade is privacy - yours."

Former Vice-President Dan Quayle fell victim to the digital loss of privacy in 1993 when Jeffrey Rothfeder, author of the book *Privacy for Sale*, accessed his credit report. He also pulled CBS-TV news anchor Dan Rather's credit report and, for good measure,

Vanna White's home telephone number. "I got it all with little difficulty," Rothfeder said.

Officials at credit reporting agencies such as TRW say that intrusions into the computerized databases that hold your private credit information are rare. Those intrusions that do occur are usually not the result of a determined hacker, but of someone who has obtained a legitimate password and the right phone number to dial.

"It's not like all privacy is gone, but there are serious problems with personal information being sold without your knowledge or consent," said Evan Hendricks, the U.S. privacy Council's Chairman. "It's about people prying into your life without asking your permission and individuals not having any power to stop them."

So what happens with all this information? Mostly it's used by telemarketers and various companies trying to discover if you're ripe to buy their products. If you buy dog food, for instance, and you send in a rebate coupon, your name may go on a computerized list that is sold to other pet companies. Before you know it your mailbox will fill with advertisements for dog food, flea soap, leashes and kennels. Older Americans on social security will find that not only their mailbox, but their telephone as well, will become active with medical and life insurance company solicitations from agencies that have tapped a computerized list. Annoying, certainly, but not really dangerous.

What is dangerous is when the person who obtains your personal information wants it for purposes other than innocuous solicitations. The impersonator, the stalker, the pedophile and the con artist all have reasons for wanting personal data on you or your family. And of course, there are others - old boyfriends/girlfriends, ex-spouses, those looking to settle a score, those wishing to blackmail you, extort money from you - all would benefit from the information they can track down about you. As Senator Edward Markey (D-Mass.) said: "We have to acknowledge that real harm can be done in a virtual world."

Not all of this information is easy to come by and some of it can only be obtained through illegal access, bribery, etc. What it really boils down to is that anyone with education and knowledge about the system can gain information about you. This isn't remarkable; it's been true for many years. What is remarkable is our ignorance of the fact that it is possible. Information Specialist John Bailey said that "nobody has to divulge anything. You have, as the saying goes, the right to remain silent.' You don't have to participate in mainstream society, buy property, have credit, etc. And, when you do, you don't have to divulge everything you're asked for."

The reality is rare enough that most of us have no need to worry about our personal data falling into the hands of a criminal or someone who wishes to do us harm. However, it's wise to know that there are databases out there containing personal information about you that you may wish to limit dissemination of. It's also wise, as Bailey pointed out, "to become informed about how your government works, what information is public, why it's public, how it's used legitimately, and most importantly for the individual who wants privacy, what options they have in divulging personal information for some official or business purpose."

Fortunately, there are ways to fight back against all of the crimes and criminals we have discussed. Much of what we will use in defense is common sense and much of it involves just going the extra mile to assure that computer criminals have a hard time cracking your system.

PART TWO

Cyber Security: Foiling Computer Criminals and Staying Safe

> *"The only system which is truly secure is one which is switched off and unplugged, locked in a titanium-lined safe, buried in a concrete bunker, and is surrounded by nerve gas and very highly paid armed guards. Even then I wouldn't stake my life on it."*
>
> - Professor Gene Spafford, Chairman,
>   Computer Science Dept.,
>   Purdue University.

You may operate under the notion that your computer system is far too small and unimportant to come under attack by a hacker, or that, because you generally mind your own business online, you'll never be harassed or pursued. You may believe that you're safe, but as Professor Spafford says, an absolutely one hundred percent secure computer system doesn't exist.

I rate computer vulnerability on a three step scale. The most vulnerable systems are those connected to networks, allowing outside access via dial-in modem. Hackers, phreaks, virus writers and every other type of computer criminal have their eyes on this type of system. The next level down are systems which are connected to other computers via modem, allowing uploads and downloads, making the computer vulnerable to viruses and to abuse. At least risk are computers which are never connected to any outside source and are generally only vulnerable to viruses from unchecked software.

Many of the tips and techniques that we'll talk about are directly applicable to computer networks and large mainframe systems, but all of these techniques are valuable even if a personal desktop computer is all that you use.

I would venture to say that there is no foolproof way to eliminate all possible threats to your computer and yourself. If there is no way, then there is no hope, right? Fortunately, this isn't true. There is hope. However, it doesn't come in the form of risk elimination, but of risk reduction.

The concept of reducing risk certainly isn't new. When we fasten our seatbelts in the family car, we're reducing the risk of being hurt in a collision, although buckling up doesn't guarantee we won't be injured. When we lock our doors before leaving for work we're reducing the risk of being robbed while we're away. Risk reduction is a chain made up of individual links - each link is another step toward greater safety. A break in any of these links provides an opening for a potential attack, an escalation of the risk factor.

LINK 1: THE HUMAN FACTOR

"Hackers rely on the ineptitude and laziness of users, who, often are the ones who provide the hole for a hacker to slip through," said a hacker I chatted with on a bulletin board. "Users are probably a system's greatest danger." Indeed, users make up the first and weakest link in the risk reduction chain - the human factor.

Human beings talk to other human beings. We certainly can't ask every company employee who comes into contact with a computer to suddenly go mute and refuse to communicate with others simply for fear of saying something that might compromise security. Unfortunately, when computer users talk they often let information slip...information that a hacker can use to gain system access. Most slips are unintentional: answering a technical question over the telephone or discussing something in idle conversation. It's easy for a hacker to phone you and pretend to be a company maintenance technician who needs your password so he can access the system and fix a problem. It's also common for users to give their password to a friend, who gives it to another friend, who uses it for purposes that are less than pure. Social engineering relies heavily on the fact that computer users are often unaware of and uninterested in system security. It falls on the system administrator to educate users about security measures and it falls on users to comply with keeping system information in-house.

A simple way to do this is to set and follow a rule that company employees should never discuss the system with anyone who is not a sysop or a sysadmin. Don't even discuss it with other users.

The system administrator should be the person a user goes to when he has a problem, not another user. This keeps information dissemination to a minimum and helps assure that it doesn't fall into the wrong hands. Remember, the first line of defense is people taking active steps. You can't just throw technology at a computer security problem and expect that alone to take care of it.

Users should be aware of the procedures for keeping account numbers and passwords secret, as well as recognizing and reporting hacker and virus activity. We'll look at these subjects in the following paragraphs.

LINK 2: SYSTEM SECURITY

Alec Muffet, author of *alt.security.faq*, an Internet file of frequently asked questions about computer security, says that "a system is only as secure as the people who can get at it."

Fortunately, computer systems generally have limited access points. A hacker or anyone else wishing to compromise the system must begin at the bottom, by getting access, before he can do anything with or to the system.

Remote network terminals located around an office building provide easy access and we'll look at keeping unauthorized users away from them in the section on physical security. The second method of access is the dial-in modem. Next to employee attacks from within, it's the most common form of intrusion.

Earlier, when we talked about our fictional friend Joe Schmoe needing to call up the Mach Aerospace company computer in order to place orders, download technical documents and other such business, we saw a perfect example of a company that must have its system hooked up to a dial-in modem. In many cases it's important for employees outside the office to be able to access the computer databases by telephone. But in some companies, the phone lines are virtually dormant, connected to the system but hardly ever used. If you don't need them for your business, get rid of them! They can be a direct route to the heart for a hacker's poison. Personal computer users - unless they're running a bulletin board system - don't have their modems set up to answer incoming calls, so this worry is eliminated.

If you must have dial-in lines, consider taking the following security precautions:

- Avoid using networks with public-access such as Tymnet and Sprintnet. 800 numbers should be avoided also.

- Connect the dial-in lines to a smaller system, keeping callers away from the mainframe and its databases. Or, transfer important information such as finances, employee records, etc., to a smaller system which does not have dial-in access.

- Restrict the hours during which the modem answers incoming calls. A system which is connected 24-hours a day, seven days a week invites intrusion late at night, early in the morning, or on weekends and holidays when no one is around to monitor activity.

- Do not list your dial-in line number in telephone books. Make hackers work if they're going to try to obtain the number; don't give it to them on a platter. Sometimes it pays not to advertise.

- Force users to go through a live switchboard operator before connecting to the computer, or at least put an answering machine-type recording on the line. This will go a long way toward keeping unauthorized users away.

- Maintain only active accounts, used by people who have a legitimate need for access. It's dangerous to leave unused accounts open on the system.

- Change default or maintenance accounts and passwords so that they don't provide an easy in for savvy hackers.

LOG-ON PROCEDURES

Almost all dial-in systems present an opening screen after connection that tells the caller what company machinery he has connected to. For instance: "Welcome to Mach Aerospace, Running Unix version xx.xx."

This opening screen is a *bad* idea. Not only does it tell a hacker or unauthorized personnel who owns the system, but it tells them exactly what software is handling the duties. Hackers know software, and giving them a name and version number is like handing over the combination to the safe.

Consider an opening screen that does nothing, absolutely nothing but remain blank. The user is required to hit the "enter" key once or twice before a system prompt pops up. That's all. No clues, no keys, just a generic prompt that says something like "name" or "account number." Once this is entered, a second prompt should appear requesting "password." A disguised opening screen is also helpful, such as: "Mach, Port 1, 22.34." A nice line to add is "sysop is present" or "entry monitoring operational."

A hacker will attempt as many different account/password combinations as the system will allow, trying to find a valid one. If a system gives him unlimited tries, he'll take advantage of that and sooner or later break in. Check the defaults and modify them if necessary to allow only two tries at entering account/password information. If a legitimate user trips on his fingers and enters the wrong account information, he should be allowed a second attempt. In some cases, a third attempt may be allowed, but this is pushing it. Twice should be sufficient. If the user can't log on in two tries, the system should kick him off - present a banner that says "incorrect password, access denied" and then drop the carrier and hang up.

If you really want to appear intimidating, include a line that says "illegal log-on attempt has been recorded and security administrator is currently being paged." Show the hacker that you have thought about security and have taken measures to defeat his attempts to hack the password.

Passwords are the keys to the city; every user has one and it's usually something easy to remember. Let's face it: unless a user logs on at least once a day he or she is not going to work very hard to remember a password. Repetition forces passwords to become part of one's memory, but infrequent use leads to forgetfulness. Users like something quick and simple, and that's just what a hacker hopes for.

Some passwords are assigned by the system administrator and some are dreamt up by individual users. Regardless, passwords should be unique to each account. Accounts with default passwords should be changed or deleted as soon as your system is up and running. If you haven't checked on default passwords and accounts, do it now.

Here are some tips on password selection:

- Avoid single character passwords. These are self-limiting and a hacker will make short work of getting past them.

- Avoid using first/last names, birthdates, social security numbers or driver's license numbers for passwords. These are too predictable and consist of easily obtained information.

- Hackers know the most common passwords that people tend to choose, so avoid commonly used words such as PASSWORD, ENTER, OPEN, COMPUTER and the like. Also avoid passwords that can be tied in to your hobbies. A scuba diver who uses DIVE as his password isn't being very imaginative; DIVE is one of the first words a hacker who knows the user's hobby will try.

- Stay away from extremely long passwords or those with long combinations of letters or numbers. Although these are the best type, they are difficult to remember and may cause you to change it to something easier to remember ...and easier for a hacker to guess.

- Select passwords which won't be found in the dictionary, such as word combinations, word letters/numbers or hyphenated combinations such as RED OLX, GERMANSAFETY, MARKETORANGE, JUSTICE 4T5, 496 TRANSIT, HUA-TJ, or NOAH-87. Hackers have been known to use dictionary programs of common words to hunt down passwords.

- Never write your password down anywhere! Books, card files, drawers, purses, wallets, wastebaskets and taped to a computer screen are all places passwords have been found. The only place you should keep your password is in your head.

No matter what passwords users end up with, system administrators should require that passwords have a finite lifetime. The Department of Defense National Computer Security Center (NCSC) recommends that passwords be changed every year. These new passwords can be assigned or user-selected combinations, but the change helps reduce the risk of password guessing. It also foils a hacker who may have access via a stolen password.

Studies done on the time required to hack a password based on length and complexity through purely random guessing at 10,000 tries per second works out to the following:

Password Length	26 characters a-z only	96 characters a-z, A-Z, 0-9 & punctuation	256 characters All ASCII characters
3	2 seconds	1 minute	27 minutes
4	60 seconds	2.35 hours	4 days
5	19 minutes	9 days	3 years
6	8.6 hours	2 years	891 years
7	9 days	238 years	2,283 centuries
8	241 days	228 centuries	584,546 centuries
9	17 years	21,945 centuries	149,643,989 centuries
10	447 years	2,106,744 centuries	38,308,861,211 centuries

If your password is a real word and the hacker runs a dictionary attack, these times are cut by 80 to 90 percent. It doesn't take a Cray supercomputer, either; a 486DX4-100 can run in excess of 10,000 tries per second. How long would your current password stand up under that kind of onslaught?

The letters and digits making up a password should not appear on the screen as the password is entered. Instead, the entry should appear as asterisks or the screen should remain blank. NCSC calls this a random overprint mask, which also helps to eliminate shoulder surfing and other prying eye techniques. Covering one hand with the other while typing in the password also helps to prevent the actual keyboard entry from being seen.

Passwords are also essential for personal desktop computers. If you keep sensitive files on your home computer, including personal information such as finances, you should think about using a password system to guard access.

An extra line of security against unauthorized entry through a computer system's front door is the callback unit. The best callback units are similar to telephone answering machines; they answer your voice call and ask you to enter a password via the touch tone pad on your phone. The unit breaks the connection and searches a database for password validity. If the unit finds that your name and password match what's in the database, it looks for a callback number. It then directs the system computer to call you at that number. At that point you must go through normal log-on procedures involving your account number and password.

The nice thing about a callback unit is that it virtually isolates the computer from those calling in. Not all callback units do this; some are connected to the computer from the first call. It also will not call back an unauthorized computer; only the number attached to your name and password is listed in its database.

On the down side, callback units require that the user be at the home or office terminal in order to receive the callback. The user must also know how to set up the modem in order to receive an incoming call. Callback units are not infallible. They can be defeated by such things as call-forwarding and by keeping the carrier open. They should not be relied upon for absolute security, but simply as an additional line of defense.

Activity monitoring by the system operator is a stop-gap measure that may reveal hacker activity. Many systems routinely log caller activity, noting who called and when. More sophisticated systems give more information: caller name or ID, the system port from which access was made, the time and length of the call, areas visited and activity undertaken during the online session. This allows better tracking of usage and can reveal non-standard user activity. Unfortunately, a caller log is only as good as the sysop who studies it for anomalies.

In the future, sophisticated biometric techniques such as voice recognition and validation, fingerprint, palm or signature verification and retinal scans will be used to assure that the only personnel gaining access to a system are authorized users. Until these features become commonplace, all we can do is isolate our systems from outside access, hide our data phone numbers and put passwords and callback units in place. These defensive measures form part of the outer screen, the security implemented for log-on procedures. The inner screen is the close-in line of defense that protects the data itself. A hacker who makes it past the outer screen or an employee with legitimate access who is bent on doing harm can do several things to your system. The three most harmful are data theft, data manipulation and setting loose viruses.

SECURING DATA FROM THEFT

Whether the hazard comes from an employee hacking from within or a hacker working from the outside, both represent the same level of danger. Both may try to get at the data on your system: to steal it, delete it, change it or corrupt it with a virus or by other means. The protection of data is all-important and it begins with securing it from theft.

Log-on procedures serve as the first line of defense against keeping unauthorized personnel away from data. But a hacker who slips through or an employee with sanctioned access should not be allowed to traipse freely through your system. There must be one or more secondary layers of defense to protect data.

Preventing unauthorized access is the first layer. Files or programs of a sensitive nature - company logs, finances, internal memos, company manuals, executive itineraries - should never be accessible to anyone without an express need to know. If it's something you don't want competitors or the press to get their hands on, it's sensitive. Limit the number of accounts which have online access to this information. An easy way to do this is to require employees or users to make a specific request for access and give the reason why they require such information. This at least allows company managers to keep track of who has access to what. That is important to know if ever a situation arises in which information is leaked outside of the company.

Users should only have access to that online information directly related to their position and duties. If an employee has no reason to look at finances, he or she shouldn't be given access to financial information on the mainframe. It's that simple. Restricting account privileges allows the system administrator to keep a fairly close rein on users. This doesn't, of course, prevent authorized users from stealing or selling sensitive data, but it reduces the risk.

For systems that are connected to the Internet, secure gateways known as firewalls provide extra protection. Firewalls are a collection of systems and routers placed at the central connection site of a network to restrict access to internal systems. The firewall forms a secure gateway through which all network connections pass, allowing them to be examined and restricted if necessary.

System administrators should watch for overused accounts or those being used at unusual times. These are tipoffs that something is going on and the account should be watched closely. Logging may be implemented to track where the user goes and what areas are being accessed. Matching these factors with the users' duties may reveal activities which indicate data theft.

As indicated earlier, unused accounts should be deleted from the system and users with multiple accounts should be discouraged. Users with no need for computer access should never be given a courtesy account, even one with low level privileges. Restricting access is one of the most basic ways of preventing data theft and should be routinely used. But a better way by far is to encrypt sensitive data.

Encryption is the means by which data is rendered unreadable by changing text into meaningless letters or numbers. Most encryption programs are software-based; users must run a program to encrypt or decode a file. You may recall as a child using a very basic form of encryption algorithm based on the letters of the alphabet and the numbers one through 26. The key to encode or decode was simple: A equals 1, B equals 2, C equals 3 and so on. Therefore, I can take my first name and encode it so that Laura becomes 12-1-21-18-1. If you know the key I'm using, you can look at the numbers and decode them easily. Imagine an entire text file encoded like this. Meaningless, unless you have the key.

The alphabet encryption method is, of course, well known, as basic as it gets; hardly what anyone would call secure. It illustrates, however, what encryption is all about. Modern encryption is infinitely more complex and provides an extremely high degree of security. It may encode text or data several times over, "layering" the file. Only someone with a matching key program would be able to run the encoded text through the decode process and end up with clear text.

One of the most widely-known encryption algorithms is DES, the Data Encryption Standard. Used until 1988 by the government for encoding classified documents, DES is based on a 56-bit key which makes decoding by trial and error a long and complicated process. DES is considered safe enough for non-classified government documents. The public key system is the most popular for civilian use and we'll talk about it in the section on e-mail security.

Encryption isn't a cure-all. There is always the threat that those with legitimate access and code keys may steal data. Again, all we can do is reduce the risks. Hackers and employees with larceny or revenge on their minds may not care to steal data at all, they may simply choose to manipulate it.

GUARDING AGAINST DATA MANIPULATION

Author Richard H. Baker calls data manipulation "one of the simplest, safest, and most common ways to commit a crime by computer." Manipulating or "diddling" data is commonly done by insiders - employees with legitimate access to financial, payroll and similar company records. This was mentioned earlier when we talked about internal hacking. Any time data in a computer is placed in the hands of clerks, technicians, programmers or others with responsibility for data entry, storage or retrieval, the potential for abuse exists. In 1994, the Government Accounting Office reported that improper payroll payments had cost the U.S. government over $7.8 million. Data entry clerks had created "ghost" soldiers who were receiving regular payments.

Some data manipulation is innocuous, the result of mistakes in input or output that look like diddling, but, in reality, are simply errors. Certainly accidental and unplanned errors outweigh malicious manipulation, but both pose a problem and need to be guarded against.

Data comparison is the simplest tactic, in which the system is programmed to compare the last computed value against the newly entered value. If the result is too far off the old value, the input is rejected and the account is flagged or an operator is alerted that a problem exists. Another method involves comparing output with input. This type of spot checking utilizing a control can quickly pick up out-of-range values. Yet another technique is to program the system to check for any clerk activity or requests outside of normal online duties, and to record computer usage times and the name or password of the clerk involved.

Much of the protection against data manipulation involves people who double check data and monitor employees' computer activities. Careful monitoring is still the best way to catch diddling. Of course, hackers and employees bent on revenge may not bother to read or diddle with your private files. They may instead want to cause larger problems on your system and the easiest way to do this is by setting lose a virus.

PROTECTION AGAINST VIRUSES

Computer viruses are not nearly as prevalent as those which affect humans. They do, however, pose a possible threat. Isolation is the best way to protect your computer from viruses, but isolation is highly impractical and inconvenient in most cases. It's like asking a person to stay indoors permanently, for fear of catching the flu; it can't be done. Viruses propagate to your system primarily through direct contact with contaminated software. So the first step in protecting your system from viruses - whether mainframe or personal computer - is to limit their exposure.

Software should always be purchased from a reliable dealer. This means a well known software or computer store, not some fellow selling disks off the back of a truck, a bargain bin some-where, or even an acquaintance who offers to share software with you. The software should always be packaged in unbroken shrink-wrapped cellophane for maximum security. Of course, viruses have been known to slip into commercial programs at the factory, or via returned software that has been repackaged and resold, but such occurrences are relatively rare. Gwen Lenker, writing in *ComputorEdge* magazine said that "the Software Publishers' Association (SPA) estimates that as much as 30 percent of all software sold as new may have been previously used." Download-ing programs from bulletin board systems is dangerous and should be avoided, as should exchanging disks with others.

Before inserting a new diskette into your disk drive and loading a new program, take a minute or two to backup your hard disk. Once a virus gets into your system, you'll wish you had clean backups of your programs and files to help you recover. I backup my files every day and though it seems compulsive, I hope that I'll be prepared if my data is ever corrupted by a virus.

All software new to your system should be checked for viruses before being introduced into your system. There are commercial anti-viral programs available that will scan for known viruses. These improve your odds of finding something before it takes hold, but an anti-viral program can't find newly created viruses. And new viruses are always being created. Take care to use the most up-to-date anti-viral program possible and keep in contact with the manufacturer so that you'll receive upgrades as new fixes are developed. Virus-checking software is far from perfect, however.

Basic virus checkers usually look for virus signatures: characteristic signs that a virus is present. These checkers can be fooled by polymorphic viruses that change signatures upon replication. For the most part, however, an acceptable level of safety can be maintained simply by scanning for known viruses. Other types of anti-viral software include preventive software that may prohibit viruses from spreading by erecting barriers in the path of program modification, and detective software that monitors events in a computer and reports suspicious occurrences to the user.

If you're conversant with computer code, looking at the actual strings of code that comprise a program can help to identify suspicious or out of place commands. Even if you're not conversant, it may be wise to look at the contents of a data file anyway. Experts say that strange messages are commonly inserted by virus writers and can be read among the code. Look at a data file with a word processing program and search for these.

Know how your computer and the programs on it work. Look for unusual actions, such as changes in screens and graphics and unanticipated disk activity. Keep a watch on the amount of available RAM (random access memory) on your system; a sudden decrease in available memory is a tip-off that something is amiss. It's a wise idea to write down or print out the file sizes of various programs and check them occasionally to see if an increase occurs. This may indicate a virus (although if you've added to the file since the last check, this indication will be false). You should know the contents of your CONFIG.SYS and AUTOEXEC.BAT files and check them for any extra or inserted lines or commands.

Whether you work on a personal computer or a company mainframe, you should know the most common signs of virus activity. They include:

- Applications don't work properly.

- Disks can't be accessed.

- Printing doesn't work correctly.

- Pull-down menus are distorted.

- File size changes for no reason.

- Date of last access does not match the last time of actual use.

- An increase in the number of files on the system when nothing has been added.

- Uncommanded disk drive activity.

- Unusual error messages.

- System slows down, freezes or crashes.

If any of these indications surface, you may have a virus. Treating it while minimizing data loss on the system is the next step.

Once a virus infects your system, everything on the system is suspect. You simply can't be sure what has been contaminated and what hasn't. Therefore a total rebuild is in order. If you've backed up your hard drive this shouldn't be a problem. If you haven't, you're going to lose valuable data.

As soon as a virus is suspected or detected, shut the system down. Use your clean back-up disk that contains bootable files (those containing the operating system files) to re-boot. Be sure the disk is write-protected so that the virus cannot copy itself to the clean disk. Restart the system from the disk and reformat your hard disk. You will lose all the data on the hard disk, but again, if you're backed up, this won't be a problem. Only original, manu-facturer-provided copies or trusted backups of all programs should be used to reload software onto your hard disk. These copies are the ones you originally purchased, copied and stored away...right?

It is possible to eradicate specific infected portions of your hard disk without a complete rebuild. Certain programs allow for this, but more harm than good may be caused by using them, so know what you're doing before you begin. In all cases, if in doubt, call in a professional.

Company mainframe computers are more vulnerable to viruses than personal systems because of the number of users who have access to them. A hacker or malicious employee can write and upload a virus and a user who uploads unchecked software can also introduce viruses into the system. All uploads should be routed to an upload directory and held for checking by the system administrator. This is true for both company computers and public bulletin board systems. Viruses can ruin your whole day! But if you practice safe computing, you can reduce your risk.

LINK 3: PERSONAL SECURITY

"In cyberspace, as in the real world, we must recognize that there will be miscreants who do not feel bound by any social obligation," said Kansas State University philosopher Maarten van Swaay. Unfortunately, his words ring true. Like any other place on earth, cyberspace has its faults. He goes on to say that "the problem is that without violating our own social standards, we will be unable to recognize miscreants until after they misbehave." What I believe van Swaay is alluding to is the faceless, voiceless nature of cyberspace. That screen before you is very easy to hide behind, but it does not give total safety to a criminal. Nor need it make victims of us.

Just as our personal safety on the streets of the real world depends to a great extent on our ability to use awareness and planning to avoid harm, so too is our safety online bolstered by being aware and taking proactive measures. Awareness and proaction are the two keys that can help us in cyberspace just as they can in the everyday world.

With the explosion of interest in the Internet and the popularity of the commercial online services, as well as locally-run bulletin board systems, more and more people are hooking up and going online. But, as in every other facet of life, there are ground rules which you should consider before you type your first message on the screen.

INFORMATION DISSEMINATION

When you open an account on any bulletin board system, you are usually required to give your name, address, telephone number and often a checking account or credit card number for billing purposes. You may also be asked for the type of computer you use, the brand of software you're running and other technical questions. This information is for administrative purposes only and is usually not given to other users. The only information other users see about you on most commercial online services is your name, ID or member number and sometimes a location identifier showing what part of the country you are in. On the Internet or local BBSs, your name (or sometimes a pseudonym, if you've chosen to use one) appear, along with the name of the BBS that your message originated from. Other than this, no information about you should be available to anyone that you meet online unless you specifically choose to give it to them.

The area where most users trip themselves up is in letting their guard down in the online environment. Communicating online is a fun, exciting, enjoyable undertaking, but it must be tempered with common sense. As van Swaay said, we won't be able to recognize miscreants until after they misbehave, so we must be on guard against them before they act. This doesn't mean becoming paranoid or treating everyone you meet online with suspicion; that only creates anxiety. But it does mean playing things a bit close to your vest.

The cardinal rule of online safety says that you must decide what you want others to know about you. You needn't, and indeed shouldn't, reveal your location, address, telephone number or any personal information. It's common for someone you meet in an online forum to offer to send you information about a mutual interest. That's what friends do. But how well do you know this person? You don't. Would you give a stranger on the street your home address? Think twice and use your good judgment.

It's easy to let out personal information online. Conversations are free-flowing and often uninhibited. You may tell friends online things that you would hesitate to tell them in person. Remember that public messages can be read by anyone passing through the forum or message area. When you type personal information or anecdotes onto the screen and hit the "send" button, you're launching that message to points unknown. You don't know who's going to read it. If you wouldn't shout it from the rooftops, don't post it online.

It's common for commercial services to have member lists available online. These usually list name, ID number, city and state. These postings are optional for the most part and you can have your name removed from the list if you choose. It's always a good idea to do so and to refrain from filling out any online member questionnaires that ask for personal information (such as hobbies) and then post it for other members to read. Choose what you want known about yourself and realize that in 99 percent of the cases nothing negative will occur as a result of the information you reveal. But it only takes once to make you wish you had been more careful.

IDENTITY HOAXES

The second rule of online safety says that people you meet online may not always tell the truth about themselves. This isn't a new or shocking idea; it's one that we deal with in our everyday lives as well. However, there's something about online communications that make people seem trustworthy and more than one person has found that the individual they have been talking with has been lying.

An online user described the kind of thing that can happen when you don't know the person on the other end of the screen:

"We met on line in February and one thing led to another. We exchanged pictures and decided to meet a month or so later. He visited me and everything clicked. We began talking about marriage and forever. We kept corresponding over the computer and were able to dial in to each other's computers. At the time I thought it was fun. I visited him in Texas and it was then that I found out some things about him that really bothered me. He had been married three times, never saw or heard from his children and described an abusive, violent childhood. He became extremely jealous as well, so I decided to slowly break off the relationship. He seemed to accept it and I thought we parted friends.

"In early June, I began a very nice friendship with a gentleman in Wisconsin. We exchanged ideas about computers and common interests. Even though he seemed to have a deeper interest in me than friendship, we kept corresponding and exchanged GIF's over the computer. Although we were only friends, a mutual trust grew between us and we shared some very personal things about one another. Then my friend in Wisconsin called me on the phone and was livid. He was reading an e-mail that he received which contained nearly all the personal information that he had shared with me, but it had been turned around in such a negative way that it appeared that I was poking fun at him rather than compassion. When I told him that I had not written it, he hung up the phone and we've not corresponded since. I tried reaching him by phone and have sent letters through the mail explaining what has happened, but to no avail. A day or so after the incident I received a short and sweet e-mail from the hacker in Texas that I had broken up with, which said simply 'Gotcha.'"

This user reported the incident to the management of the online service, but they told her that they could do nothing about it and recommend that she close her account and reactivate it in a few months under a new screen name.

"Even though the service monitored my usage and saw that someone was signing on under my screen name during times that I was at work, they still didn't consider that proof that I didn't reveal my password to someone. They absolved themselves of all responsibility. I have had to change my phone number twice because of this guy. He was able to get my previous phone number from e-mails that I had sent to a few of my friends. In my opinion, this is a form of stalking, especially when my phone used to ring in the middle of the night - all night."

This user now realizes that "meeting online (especially when there was so much distance between two people) is somewhat unconventional and that in the future I will not take these online relationships more seriously than friendship."

Little white lies are more common, as are embellishments and boasting of one's employment or social position. We all want to appear important, we all want to "be somebody." Unfortunately, when we're online, we can be anybody and only someone who knows us personally would know the difference.

Take most things with a grain of salt. Don't take financial advice from someone online who claims to be an advisor, or legal advice from someone who claims to be a lawyer. Don't send money or reveal your credit card number to anyone online. If you must do business with someone you've met online, get a telephone number from them and speak with them directly before you make any decisions. Be wary of who you give personal information to. It just isn't wise to do this with someone you've met only online.

Beware of electronic mail messages asking for personal information. System administrators should never ask you for your address or phone number, they should already have it from your sign-on. Absolutely no one should ever ask you for your password. There is no one - aside from you - who needs that information. If you're ever asked - either online or through a personal telephone call - for your password or other personal information by someone who purports to be a staff member of an online service or BBS, immediately send a message or call the sysop or customer service and alert them. If the request came in the form of an e-mail message, forward a copy of the message as well.

Remember that there is no law that says you must reply to a message you receive. You are fully within your rights to ignore it, delete it or refuse to give the sender the information requested. You are also free to demand further identification. Confronting the sender often forces him to back down. Take control of your online life: when in doubt, check it out.

ONLINE HARASSMENT AND STALKING

Threatening or harassing public or e-mail messages are uncalled for and often against the rules. Depending on the service or BBS you use, the rules may allow a wider latitude of conduct, so make it a point to be aware of this. You don't have to respond to messages that are argumentative, threatening or harassing. The sender is usually looking for a response. Don't give him one. This in itself may be enough to make him cease. If it isn't, report the messages to the sysop or customer service.

On the Internet, where control over message content is minimal at best, there is no "higher authority" to which you can report transgressions. In this case, ignoring the harassing messages is of paramount importance. Again, the sender is looking for a response and the failure to get one may be enough to send him elsewhere. In extreme cases you may wish to move to another message base. Avoidance, too, is a wise choice.

Stalking via e-mail is rare, but when it does occur it can be terribly unsettling. Here again, ignoring the messages is best. If the messages continue or are of a threatening nature, save the messages and forward them to customer service if you use a commercial online service. If the e-mail comes via an Internet connection, your best bet is to contact your local law enforcement agency for assistance. Never take chances.

PROTECTING CHILDREN ONLINE

Computer use by children has always been a touchy issue and never more so than when the news media began to report stories of children being lured by online pedophiles. The articles were frightening. Many a parent has considered cutting off all online access for their children, rather than take a chance of having their child endangered. While it is true that there have been cases of pedophiles seducing children thorough computer services, the incidents themselves should be considered fairly rare. With proper education, the risk to your child can be drastically reduced.

A child with a computer and a modem, tucked away behind closed doors, is an unknown entity. Parental supervision is vital.

In fact, I won't hesitate to say that it is the single most important action you can take to protect your child in the online environment.

In the U.S. House of Representatives, Reps. Christopher Cox (R-Calif.) and Ron Wyden (D-Ore.) said that parents and families - not government - should "guard the portals of cyberspace." Sit with your children as they use their computers, ask them questions about what they find online and who they talk to there. Most children are thrilled to be able to share their knowledge of the computer world with adults. Show your interest and make time to join them in their online activities.

Don't be afraid to ask your children if they have ever received any strange or sexually suggestive messages. Ask them how they handled the situation. Tell them that they should share these messages with you, no matter how embarrassing they are. And be sure they know that they will never be reprimanded for doing so. Make it quite clear that responding to such messages is a bad idea, but if they admit that they have, be sure to find out how many times they have exchanged messages with the individual and what information they have given out.

Children should be instructed never to reveal personal information such as their address, telephone number, and name or location of their school. The National Center for Missing and Exploited Children recommends that children never send a person their picture or anything else without first checking with their parents and receiving permission.

The NCMEC also recommends that children pledge never to agree to meet face-to-face with someone they only know online without first checking with their parents. If you decide to allow your child to meet someone whom they've only talked to online, the meeting should take place in a public place and a parent should go along. A child should never meet someone alone.

Parents should set up rules about online activities that include the time of day and length of time a child can be online, and make clear what areas are off-limits and are not to be visited. Check with your online service about restricting access to adult-oriented sections of commercial services. This is usually possible and simple to implement. Also emerging are new software filters that allow parents to prevent their children from accessing certain Internet sites and which also screen for offensive materials. Check with your local computer software store for details.

Children don't have to fear the online world; with parental concern and involvement, they can enjoy the information super-highway without getting run off the road.

MAINTAINING PRIVACY

"If there's anything people need to understand, it's that they are responsible for their protection, both privacy and personal. They cannot assign that responsibility to the government. The harder they try to do that, the less safe and less private they will be," said Information Specialist John Bailey. He knows what the rest of us sometimes prefer to deny: that it takes action by each of us to remain safe and maintain our privacy.

Most of the information that is "out there" about an individual has been willingly released by that individual. Recently, while going about the quite routine business of renewing my library card I was asked to fill out a form which asked for my name, address, telephone number and social security number. Now why would a library need my social security number? Here is a prime example of an individual's ability to limit information dissemination. In most cases, you can simply say "no, that's private information." Just leave the space blank. I don't think I'm in any danger by allowing the library to have my SSN, but if they place it in a database, who knows who can get to it. I don't want that. I would rather have as much control as possible of the information about me.

John Bailey, who talked to me at length about privacy, said that it is "neither possible nor desirable to live in such a way that your private information is secure. One would have to live in a cabin in the mountains - make that a rented cabin, or you'd be in the property records. You wouldn't want to have any kind of job or income or you'd make tax records, etc. If you want privacy in your medical records, refuse to sign the insurance form - of course, then, you need to have enough money to be self-insured. And, where would you put that amount of money? Every check you write or cash is microfilmed and stored for up to seven years. Anyone determined enough to get your records, whatever those are, can get them. Just as anyone determined enough to defeat a vault or any other security measures can do so."

This type of privacy invasion is rare. According to Bailey, "the cyber crime that the individual really has to worry about involves using the computer to obtain information about the individual. Most of the time, this is done by using the computer as a teletype to communicate with and con the victim, rather than to research them through databases. Criminals are both lazy and cheap, otherwise they'd have a real job. They don't want to pay the sign-up fee and they don't want to bother to learn how to use the systems required to really do an effective job of intelligence gathering."

Regardless, there is much that we can do to audit our privacy vulnerability. A good general guideline suggested by Bailey is to first obtain a copy of the Public Record Statutes for your state, and a copy of the Federal Freedom of Information code. Read these closely, and make notes about all the records that exist - not just the ones that are known to be public.

Second, consider and make a list of all the other records that you generate in the course of your life. This includes telephone bills, bank transactions, credit cards, employment and earnings, tax returns, and the like. Obtaining bank statements, credit card transactions and phone records is a matter of routine for any good investigator, so none of these things are truly private. Each of these records should be reviewed with an eye toward how they could expose you to harm. And harm, says Bailey, "means every-thing from embarrassment to stalking to murder."

Next, start from the top of your list with public records first, then closed ones - and get a copy of everything. Do this in person as much as possible, and always ask "what else can I get?" and "where else can I look?" Then, sort all the information into the following categories: harmful (exposes you directly), potentially harmful (leads to exposure, or insinuates other facts), benign (does not appear to expose or lead to exposure), and finally, helpful (misleading, though not potentially embarrassing).

As I stated earlier, we willingly generate and release more information about ourselves than we could imagine possible. Analyze the human factor, and understand the points of information dissemination. Learn what not to put in the garbage can, and what not to tell people about your plans, business, finances, family, etc. In order of obvious priority, make notes about how to conceal, destroy, or change harmful or potentially harmful information, while increasing the volume of helpful information, especially in public sources. Bailey says that "this is where you have to really make notes, think ahead, and be careful not to violate any laws. An attorney should review the entire strategy before any of it gets put into place."

Finally, work your strategy and then start all over to audit your effectiveness, preferably using a different expert investigator. Where do you find an investigator? Criteria for a privacy audit is really a matter of perspective, but Bailey suggests that you need someone who does a lot of database research, and perhaps has done investigative work in the jurisdiction where you live and work. You would definitely want to avoid the neighborhood PI in favor of someone who has a bonafide background in personal protection and counter intelligence work. The "privacy-peddling bananas" who shout and generally draw attention to the public's lack of privacy, should be avoided if possible. Experts say that they're out to shock and frighten, not inform.

E-MAIL SECURITY

For the computer user, online privacy really comes down to one point: electronic mail. E-mail is becoming more and more popular; a quick way to deliver messages without using an envelope, a stamp and the U.S. mail. Personal messages, important files, legal documents and more now take the electronic road, and keeping these messages private is a concern. Andre Bacard, author of *The Computer Privacy Handbook*, says "Show me an e-mail user who has no financial, sexual, social, political, or professional secrets to keep from his family, his neighbors, or his colleagues, and I'll show you someone who is either an extraordinary exhibitionist or an incredible dullard. Show me a corporation that has no trade secrets or confidential records, and I'll show you a business that is not very successful."

Unlike a letter in a envelope, the contents of which are effectively invisible to the postal workers through whose hands it passes, electronic mail can be read by anyone at any of the way stations between the originating computer and the destination computer. The question of whether anyone actually does read e-mail that isn't addressed to them is moot - we put our paper mail in envelopes don't we? Our electronic mail should bear the same protection. Unfortunately, it doesn't. But the capability to protect it exists for anyone; it's called encryption.

As described earlier, encryption is a means of rendering text unreadable by anyone who does not possess the proper decryption key. Bruce Schneier, in his book *e-Mail Security*, wrote that "a key is a random bit string - sometimes a number, sometimes a value, or sometimes a word or phrase - that is used in conjunction with an algorithm...Each different key causes the algorithm to work in a slightly different way." For example, I write a message to you and encrypt it with an algorithm and key. When you receive the message, you use a decryption algorithm and the same key to render the message readable. If you don't have the key you can't decrypt and read the message, it's as simple as that.

No algorithm is completely secure, except possibly for the one-time pad (in which the algorithm is used only once and completely changed for the next message). "An attack," Schneier says, "is always possible; there is no way to prevent it. The best one can do is to make the attack so expensive, both in time and money, that no one would even consider launching it." DES - the Data Encryption Standard - for instance, has 70 quadrillion possible keys. It would take a computer capable of one million trials per second, 1,142 years to calculate all the keys.

Unfortunately, there are problems with encrypting messages in the logical way. Both the sender and the receiver, for instance, have to know the key and a different key must be used for each sender and receiver. This can get complicated, to say the least. This problem, fortunately, is solved through what's known as public key cryptography.

Put simply, each message encrypted with a public key algorithm is given its own special key. Each message is sent with a randomly-generated key, so if I were to discover the key used for a message of yours I intercepted, it would only be good for decrypting that particular message, not the next one you send, which would use a different randomly-generated key. Public key cryptography doesn't use a shared key and therein lies the beauty of it. In public key cryptography, as it relates to you and me, an encryption key and a decryption key exist; the decryption or private key is secret and it's my job to keep it that way. The encryption key is public and that's the key I distribute to all and sundry. If you'd like to send an encrypted message to me, you first find out my public key and use it to encrypt your message to me. When I get the message, I use my private key to decrypt the message. No one who intercepts the message can decrypt it without using my private key. If I'm smart, I'll guard my private key with just about everything short of my life.

A commonly used program to encrypt e-mail using public key cryptography is Pretty Good Privacy, or PGP. Created by Boulder, Colorado software engineer Philip Zimmerman in 1991, PGP was released to the computer community as free software and soon became, and remains, probably the worldwide de facto standard for e-mail encryption. It's available free through the Internet and anyone can use it. There are other public key encryption programs also, such as PEM, but none as well-known as PGP.

Encryption for e-mail is not as widely used as it should be, especially among the public. Government agencies routinely encrypt messages, but their need for security is far greater than ours. Even if you don't believe someone is reading your e-mail, you should still take steps to secure your electronic communications just as we secure our paper communications.

A sidebar to the encryption issue is anonymous remailers. Remailers allow anyone to send e-mail or newsgroup messages anonymously. *Time* magazine's Joshua Quittner called remailers "the network equivalent of a Swiss bank." On the Internet, each message carries the electronic address of the sender; unfortunately, this is a drawback if you're seeking to remain anonymous. A remailer strips the address from your message, replaces it with a random address and sends it on to its destination. The recipient never knows who the sender is, though he can post his reply in care of your anonymous address. It's the ultimate in mail forwarding and although it doesn't provide for message security, it does provide identity security.

LINK 4: PHYSICAL SECURITY

For the personal computer user, the physical security of the computer sitting on the desktop is fairly simple: you tell the kids to keep their mitts off of it, you password-protect any private or financial files and you lock the doors and windows to your house. That's it, that's physical security.

For a network or a company mainframe however, physical security must, by necessity, go a good deal further. The need for and extent of physical security must be determined on a case-by-case basis and is beyond the scope of this book. Only a qualified computer security consultant can evaluate your particular system and determine what measures your company needs to take. What follows is a quick look at physical security.

PHYSICAL ACCESS CONTROLS

If a person cannot get to your computer system, he cannot make use of what it contains. Access control is the first of the physical security barriers, the fence around the perimeter of your property.

In a network situation, where there are computers on almost every desk in the company, access control can be difficult at best. Procedural techniques like passwords and limitations on account privileges work best here. Employees should never allow anyone else - employee, friend, relative, or total stranger - to use their computer, and should always lock their offices when they leave, even if only for a short time. In situations where the main computer facilities are located in a separate and dedicated room, access control becomes even more important.

Advertising the location of the computer facility is not a good idea. Those who need to know how to get there should be given directions or be escorted, and those who don't need to know shouldn't be shown the way by signs or directory listings. Other than authorized personnel whose job it is to maintain the system, very few employees should ever need to visit the main computer facility.

All computer rooms should utilize single point access procedures. In other words: one way in and one way out. Cut down your vulnerability by reducing the number of access points. For best control, a guard or other employee should be posted at the door. Token-based authentication is a commonly used technique. It requires the user to produce proof in the form of a token which identifies the employee as a legitimate user. Identification badges are an example of these and should be mandatory. ID's should be checked against the guard's master list before access is permitted. ID cards come in various forms, from those with magnetic strips to those that carry miniature transmitters. Unfortunately, badges can be forged. This is where biometrics come in.

For companies that can afford it, higher levels of identification employing more sophisticated technology can be used. Biometric authentication involves measuring personal attributes such as a voice, fingerprint, retina, or signature. These are much more difficult to forge, but are often cost prohibitive. A combination of token-based authentication, plus biometrics is a good way to increase the level of security.

Log-in sheets are mandatory as a means of keeping track of who entered the room, at what time and for how long. Sign-in and sign-out should be required to provide for audits in case of data loss. In addition, careful audits of what users bring in and what they take out may reduce loss through data leakage.

Access control is not perfect and never will be. It is compromised by remote terminals, employees who fail to do their jobs, and general carelessness. The National Computer Security Center calls access control discretionary "in the sense that a user or process given discretionary access to information is capable of passing that information along to another subject." You can make access difficult, but you can never make it impossible.

SITE HARDENING

Any computer, whether it's the Macintosh on your desktop or the VAX at corporate headquarters, needs to be protected from attacks that don't come from a fast-fingered hacker or an insider diddling the data. Threats such as fire, power failures and system crashes are much more common and must be guarded against.

The main computer itself should be housed in a building constructed of fire-resistant and non-combustible materials. The computer facility should be separated from adjacent areas by non-combustible fire-resistant partitions, walls, and doors. All backup tapes and disks need to be outside the computer room in a separate, secure, fire-resistant area. Floors and ceilings should be checked to see that they are constructed of non-combustible materials. All computer room personnel should be trained in basic fire-fighting techniques, as well as personal safety and evacuation methods.

The computer facility itself should be protected by one or more of the following features: automatic carbon dioxide, halogen agent, water sprinklers, or wet pipe. Portable fire extinguishers should be located in easy-to-find, marked areas. Smoke detectors should be installed in ceilings, under raised flooring, and in air return ducts for maximum protection. All employees should be aware of the location of emergency power shutdown controls and how to use them. Fire drills, conducted regularly, help keep escape skills sharp.

Electronic components heat up, melt down and catch fire occasionally. Keeping your system cool requires assuring that your computer or mainframe resides in a well-ventilated, air-conditioned area. Fans and other vents on the equipment should be checked to see that they are not blocked by walls, cabinets, other devices, or dust. A fire extinguisher should be mounted within easy reach, or at least within a few steps of workstations.

Raised flooring should have adequate drainage, with drains installed on the floor to divert water away from hardware. Electrical junction boxes should be located off the slab floor to prevent water overflow from adjacent areas from reaching them. Exterior windows, doors and ceilings should be checked for water integrity and leaks. Always have large plastic sheets available to cover equipment in cases leaks or accidental sprinkler discharges occur.

Power supplies for both personal computers and mainframes should have adequate surge, spike, transient and lightning strike protection, as well as uninterruptable backup power to run the equipment in case of a power failure. If doors work on cipher locks, they should be backed up with batteries, as should fire alarms. All data on hard disks should be backed up daily and the backups stored in a separate room.

How to Protect Yourself from Computer Criminals

Cyber-Cops:
Walking the Digital Beat

"There are good guys who are still smarter than bad guys."

- U.S. Army MP David Kennedy
Information Systems Security

C yberspace is many things, but one thing it is not is perfect. Some have called the virtual world controlled chaos, while others - like myself - believe it to be a modern version of the wild West. Whatever you call it and whatever you believe it to be, cyberspace is unquestionably the hottest thing around. Everyone is talking about it and it seems nearly everyone is visiting it. And as more and more people create a sort of second life for themselves online, they will find that, much like the real world, there are criminals in this place.

Wherever there is an opportunity for profit there is bound to be a criminal around to attempt to acquire it illegally. The virtual world is not immune from this simple fact. However, those who choose to break the speed limit on the Information Superhighway must be prepared for a possible encounter with the cyber cops, that growing band of law enforcers whose lights in the virtual rearview mirror are a hacker's worst nightmare.

The first unwritten rule of hacking is "don't get caught." Dave Kennedy, U.S. Army Information Systems Security said, "The only bad guys we ever catch are either unlucky or make mistakes. The bad guys who are lucky and don't make mistakes commit the perfect crime, but they also can get arrogant and that's their mistake." Hackers are inveterate braggers; they talk about their exploits, they write about their best hacks, they natter endlessly to other hackers, and they may eventually get careless.

"A hacker's primary protection lies in his anonymity," a hacker once wrote. "Those who live the high profiles are the ones who take the fall." Kevin Mitnick is a perfect example of a hacker who got arrogant, stepped over the line, broke all the rules and finally, simply underestimated those whose systems he hacked and the abilities of the cyber cops. In the end this combination was his downfall.

Mitnick was thirty-one when he was arrested in early 1995, but his hacking career had begun much earlier, in his days as a student at Monroe High School in California. It was here that he began to compile his curriculum vitae, breaking into the Los Angeles Unified School District computers and the mainframes of the North American Air Defense Command. The break-ins were simple pranks and demonstrated Mitnick's knack for cracking even the most complex systems.

Mitnick's first conviction came when he decided to steal Pacific Bell computer manuals, but time behind bars wasn't enough to deter him; in 1988 he was convicted again, this time of accessing long distance codes on MCI Telephone Company computers. But the addiction that sometimes characterizes hacking kept driving Mitnick, and in 1994 he was under investigation by the FBI for computer-related crimes and was sought by the United States Marshal's Service for violating an earlier parole. His mother said he feared being arrested and serving prison time. But, again, even with law enforcement at his heels he couldn't stay away from hacking. This time, however, his target would hack back.

In late 1994, security expert Tsutomu Shimomura received a call from colleagues at the San Diego Supercomputing Center. Someone, they told him, had accessed his personal computer, which was connected to the Center's network. This person had read Shimomura's private e-mail and downloaded security-related files and software. Meanwhile, up the coast at the San Francisco-based online service called the Well, system administrators were puzzling over an increase in file storage in a section of the network belonging to a group called Computers, Freedom and Privacy. Bruce Koball, a group organizer and computer programmer, checked the directory and found Shimomura's files there.

Shimomura decided to take action. Recruiting several colleagues, he set up a monitoring operation to track the intruder. By now a profile had emerged and Shimomura and his team were sure that the hacker they were chasing was Kevin Mitnick. It didn't take them long to discover that Mitnick had stolen nearly twenty thousand credit card numbers from members of Netcom, an Internet provider. This brought Shimomura and his team to Netcom's headquarters in San Jose, where, with the help of U.S. Assistant Attorney General Kent Walker, subpoenas disclosed telephone records which revealed that Mitnick had been connecting to the company from dial-in lines in Minneapolis, Denver and Raleigh. Netcom engineers found that their Raleigh, North Carolina switching station had been electronically tampered with, indicating a possible location for Mitnick.

Shimomura, now working with police, the FBI and Sprint Cellular technicians, flew to Raleigh and tracked Mitnick's cellular calls to an apartment complex. FBI special agents went to work and further narrowed the search down to an apartment, for which they obtained a federal search warrant. At 1:30 a.m. FBI agents stood in the rain and knocked on the door to Apartment 202. Mitnick answered. Perhaps the most sought-after computer criminal of our time had finally been caught.

Shimomura is considered something of a hero for tracking down Mitnick, but in fact it was a team effort involving him and various law enforcement agencies, including the FBI and the U.S. Marshal's Office. Because computer crime is not epidemic (yet) online policing is a new venture. There aren't many computer cops out there because, even though there are federal laws and laws in 49 of the 50 states that apply to computers, technological crime isn't a priority. Violent street crime takes precedence, and so cyberspace is still very much a wild West. However, as computers become tools for more and more hackers and other criminals, law enforcement agencies across the country are gradually recognizing the need to become cyber cops.

A National Institute of Justice survey conducted in 1986 found that 75 percent of the police chiefs surveyed and 63 percent of the sheriffs said computer crime investigations were likely to have a significant impact on their workloads in the future. The percentages were even higher in areas with populations of 500 thousand residents or more: 84 percent of police chiefs and 75 percent of sheriffs.

Responding to the need for computer crime enforcement, the City of Los Angeles Police Department established a computer crime unit. In Philadelphia, police officers in the city's Economic Crime Unit now investigate computer crime, and in Colorado, the Denver and Lakewood city governments have instituted a joint task force to deal with the problem.

Dedicated computer crime units are still a relative rarity; it's often difficult for departments to find officers with the education and expertise in computers to be effective. Taking these officers from the streets, where they are most needed, and placing them behind computers is almost impossible, so the officers that make up most computer crime units serve dual purposes: they work both the real streets and the streets of cyberspace. Often, they receive help from civilians who serve as modern day virtual bounty hunters.

In Kevin Mitnick's case it was Tsutomu Shimomura who played a major role in bringing him to justice. Shimomura isn't a cop, he's a computer security expert. Angered at the break-in, he decided to put his expertise to work and do something about it. It was his skill at a keyboard, tracing ethereal connections, that proved vital to law enforcement. Near the end, as the net tightened around Mitnick's location, Shimomura was assisted by technicians from Sprint Cellular; they weren't cops either, but their assistance was essential in tracking down Mitnick's cellular calls.

In 1995, a Wisconsin private investigator spent nine months online posing as a 14-year old girl to lure a pedophile on the Internet. Appalled at the exchanges she was seeing online, the PI posted a message saying that she was "Jessica," a 14-year old who thought that "older guys treat you grown-up." This statement attracted Bryan Sisson, a 45-year old convicted pedophile. "Jessica" and

Sisson began exchanging e-mail and within a few weeks the PI, posing as Jessica, called in the FBI. After months of communicating and sending explicit pictures, Sisson arranged to meet "Jessica" in a Milwaukee hotel room. On his arrival, FBI special agents arrested him for traveling across state lines for the purpose of engaging in a sexual act with a minor.

Perhaps the most well-known civilian "cyber cop" is Clifford Stoll, author of *The Cuckoo's Egg*. Stoll, an astrophysicist at the Lawrence Berkeley Laboratory in California, had been working in the lab's computer section after budget cuts forced him from his position in the astronomy section. A 75-cent computer accounting error led Stool to a hacker who turned out to be part of an international spy ring. Stoll joined forces with special agents of the FBI and National Security Agency (NSA) to help crack the ring. It's a rollicking good story that proves that not all cyber cops wear badges.

POLICING THE INFO HIGHWAY

Newsweek's Michael Meyer wrote that "it's no accident that cyber crime is surging. Everyone these days seems to be buying PC's and getting wired." And therein lies the problem.

As cyberspace grows, so does the need to have a law enforcement presence to deal with the increase in high-tech crime. Cyberspace is an entirely new realm for law enforcement, a strange and sometimes alien environment which doesn't fit the normal way in which police fight crime. Clyde M. Stites, commander of the Multnomah County, Oregon Sheriff's Office detective division, writing in *Law and Order* magazine, said that "the hot crime tool for the '90s is the personal computer...police are encountering personal computers used in money laundering, narcotics sales and prostitution rings."

These days, computers aren't just the domain of hackers. They are increasingly being used much like notebooks to record everything from a drug trafficker's buyers to a prostitute's appointments and a bookie's point spreads. Ramzi Yousef, accused in the 1993 New York World Trade Center bombing, is said to have stored encrypted information on the hard drive of his laptop computer. "For the well-trained law enforcement officer," said Stites, "information stored in computers represents a new gold mine of information."

Michael R. Anderson, an IRS Criminal Investigation Division Special Agent, said "information stored in a computer is as volatile as the flash paper used in bookie operations." Extracting this type of evidence from computers is becoming a science all its own, known in law enforcement circles as "computer forensics."

Police are used to dealing with solid physical evidence, not the bits and bytes, the minutiae of information stored on hard drives and floppy disks. Technology, however, is forcing them to become educated in this new specialty. Dr. David L. Carter, a professor at the School of Criminal Justice at Michigan State University wrote in the *FBI Law Enforcement Bulletin* that "a computer crime can occur in three milliseconds using a program code that tells the software to erase itself after the computer executes the action. Essentially, this eliminates the evidentiary trail."

An investigator must be able to show evidence to establish the offense. In effect: no evidence, no crime. And even if evidence is recovered "electronic data interchange and its networks complicate the legal elements by making it more difficult for law enforcement to specify, document and materially link the crime to an individual," said Dr. Carter.

The Federal Bureau of Investigation Academy at Quantico, Virginia, now teaches classes in computer crime investigation and evidence collection, as does the Federal Law Enforcement Training Center (FLETC) at Glynco, Georgia. The state of Florida, considered a trend setter in computer crime enforcement, has a Computer Evidence Recovery Unit to process seized computers and Brevard County's Law Enforcement Electronic Technical Assistance Committee (LEETAC) travels across the state assisting in computer seizures.

There are innovations, too, in the law enforcement response to online crime. Police officers have been known to set up "sting boards" - bulletin board systems run by an undercover officer. In much the same way as prostitutes or drug dealers are caught by police working undercover, cops online pose as hackers, teenagers, or any other guise they may need to lure criminals, collect evidence on them and eventually effect an arrest. Entire bulletin boards have been set up solely for sting purposes, while in other cases, lone officers like San Jose's Detective Jim McMahon have gone trolling on their own, alone on the electronic streets. It's policing gone high tech, where a cop's computer expertise is valued almost as much as his street sense.

Despite the law enforcement leaps toward keeping up with high-tech crime, there are still victims. Computer systems are still cracked by hackers and data is still lost to these thieves. And despite the slow recognition of computer-related crime, there are very few police officers trained in this arcane art.

"The sad truth is that the FBI has less than ten agents trained in the processing of computer evidence. The Secret Service has fewer," said IRS Special Agent Anderson. "Traditionally, law enforcement at all levels has been more reactionary. That has worked for hundreds of years. The problem with technology is that it changes too quickly and law enforcement has to stay current or the technology curve will leave them in the dust."

Keeping abreast of new problems, new issues in computer security and new solutions is vital, as is a citizen's responsibility to report computer crime so that others can potentially be saved from becoming victims.

REPORTING COMPUTER CRIME

Cyberspace is nothing if not a burgeoning community, and like any community, it must come together against crime. Information exchange is a prime way in which computer users, network managers, bulletin board operators, software engineers and others meet the challenges of computer security.

One of the leaders in security-related advisories is CERT, the Computer Emergency Response Team. CERT was formed by the Defense Advanced Research Projects Agency in November, 1988 in response to the Internet worm incident. CERT works with the Internet community to facilitate its response to computer security events involving Internet hosts, to take proactive steps to raise the community's awareness of computer security issues, and to conduct research targeted at improving the security of existing systems.

To this end CERT provides 24-hour technical assistance for responding to computer security incidents, product vulnerability assistance, technical documents, and seminars. In addition, the team maintains mailing lists and a USENET newsgroup for CERT advisories. A CERT advisory, according to the team "provides information on how to obtain a patch or details of a workaround for a known computer security problem." CERT works closely with vendors to produce workarounds or patches for security problems.

If you come up against a security break-in, virus or other computer security problem, you are encouraged to contact the CERT Coordination Center at their e-mail address: cert@cert.org, or call their 24-hour hotline at (412) 268-7090 (FAX 412-268-6989). CERT personnel answer from 7:30 a.m. to 6:00 p.m. eastern time and are on call for emergencies during other hours. Or you may wish to photocopy, fill out and send in the CERT Incident Reporting Form located in the appendix of this book. Security-related information is also available through Internet anonymous FTP at cert.org.

But what if you've lost data to a hacker or discovered that someone has been siphoning off funds from accounts receivable? Aren't these crimes that can be prosecuted, not just reported? They are indeed.

"Readers need to understand that if they fall prey to a computer crime, they can't just call the FBI or the Secret Service and have an agent at their doorstep in a matter of minutes. If you call either of these agencies today, chances are that, at best a clerk will write up a report that will never be read," says Special Agent Anderson.

"The majority of law enforcement folks trained to deal with computer-related evidence (about 500-600 in North America) work with computer evidence that involves the computer used as a tool to commit a crime. Drug dealers use computers to track profits, payables and distribution. Murderers use computers to store their diaries. Computers are the ideal tool for financial frauds. Also, the computer itself is a target for theft. When that happens valuable data can be lost forever if it hasn't been backed up and stored in a place away from the computer. The FBI isn't staffed or equipped to deal with such investigations. Local, county and state law enforcement agencies are, in many cases, and they are the ones you should turn to 99 percent of the time."

Anderson says that persistence is paramount. "You may get the brush off, but chances are that either the local police, county sheriff or state police will be able to help you preserve the evidence and either investigate or refer the case."

Computer-related crime, like any other type of crime, requires our active work to reduce. As computers become more prevalent, the problem will surely continue. It's up to us to assist law enforcement in making the more unsavory residents of cyberspace toe the line.

Closing Thoughts

> *"The world isn't run by weapons anymore, or energy, or money. It's run by ones and zeros - little bits of data - it's all electrons...There's a war out there, a world war. It's not about who has the most bullets, it's about who controls the information - what we see and hear, how we work, what we think. It's all about information."*
>
> \- From the movie "Sneakers"
> MCA/Universal Pictures, 1992

My personal introduction to the world of computers coincided closely with the explosion of the hacker phenomenon. Driven by the computer attacks of the 414 Gang, the release of the 1984 movie "War Games," Steven Levy's book *Hackers* and the birth of the hacking group Legion of Doom, the early 1980's felt like a boiling kettle of computer mischief. As a high school student taking a computer science class, I heard bits and pieces of all this, and I remember being sternly lectured by my instructor that computers were not toys, they were tools. And like all tools, you had to learn how to use them properly or you might do harm. Students were forbidden to bring in any floppy disks from outside the classroom. Our terminals had no modems and could only access certain portions of the class mainframe. The mainframe itself resided behind a locked door and to this day I can't recall ever having actually seen it. It was cool stuff indeed and we all secretly dreamed of hacking it, but none of us had the courage to try.

Regrettably, I have forgotten much of what I learned in that high school class, but I can never forget the stories of viruses and hackers and the things computers could do in the hands of those skilled enough to manipulate them.

It was more than twelve years before I came to write about what I had only been told about in school. And in over a dozen years behind a keyboard, visiting cyberspace, I have, fortunately, never been a victim of a computer criminal. I have, however, touched the fringes of that world. There was the fellow who decided to send me nasty e-mail messages after seeing my messages posted on a Christian music forum. He said he was an atheist and judging by the language he used and the opinions he expressed, I don't doubt that he was. I broke my own rule and ignored my best judgment by replying to him, trying to get him to see the other side. He backed down and I never heard from him again. I'm sure he's still out there somewhere, probably harassing somebody else. There have been other minor incidents on my cyber road, but I've been extremely lucky. I'm a cyber resident who has managed thus far to avoid the bad parts of "town" and I'd like to keep it that way.

Cyberspace has so much to offer and so far yet to go. Dr. Fred Cohen said it best: "You are probably going to have to get on the information superhighway if you want to get anywhere in the information age, and there are going to be accidents and crimes on that highway just as there are accidents and crimes on our automotive highways. There are no safety belts in most modern computers, and the computer criminals know how to break into your computer over the network just as their compatriots know how to break into your car in a parking lot." Our safety depends on educating ourselves about the threats and taking active measures against them, just as we do in the real world when we lock our doors and avoid walking alone at night.

We can be safe in cyberspace; safe to open up the throttle and race across the virtual landscape, absorbing and enjoying the brave new world just beyond our keyboards.

>   - Laura E. Quarantiello
>   CompuServe: 73733,1653
>   Internet: 73733.1653@compuserve.com

Appendix

RESOURCES FOR MORE INFORMATION

COMPUTER EMERGENCY RESPONSE TEAM
Coordination Center
Software Engineering Institute
Carnegie Mellon University
Pittsburgh, PA 15213
Voice #: 412-268-7090
E-Mail: cert@cert.org

Promotes computer security through proactive measures. Central repository for information on technical problems and system-wide breaches and attacks.

FEDERAL BUREAU OF INVESTIGATION
National Computer Crime Squad
J. Edgar Hoover FBI Building
10th and Pennsylvania Avenue
Washington, DC 20535
Unit Chief: (202) 324-3283

Interstate crimes, federal interest computer crimes and international incidents.

UNITED STATES SECRET SERVICE
Electronic Crimes Branch
1800 G. Street, Room 900
Washington, DC 20223
Voice: 202-435-5850

Computer crimes involving federal interest computers and general intrusions.

NATIONAL INSTITUTE OF STANDARDS AND TECHNOLOGY
U.S. Department of Commerce
Computer Systems Laboratory
Technology Building, B151
Gaithersburg, MD 20899-0001
Voice: (301) 948-1784
E-mail: dward@enh.nist.gov (to subscribe to CSL bulletins)

Security publications, technical support for information technology, developing industry standards for computer technology.

NATIONAL CENTER FOR MISSING AND EXPLOITED CHILDREN
2101 Wilson Boulevard, Suite 550
Arlington, Virginia 22201-3052

Provides information on online child safety, missing children and child abuse.

INTERACTIVE SERVICES ASSOCIATION
8403 Colesville Road, Suite 865
Silver Spring, MD 20910

Information on interactive services and online safety.

ELECTRONIC FRONTIER FOUNDATION
1001 G Street NW, Suite 950 E
Washington, DC 20001
Voice: (202) 347-5400
Internet: info@eff.org

Nonprofit public interest membership group working to protect individual rights in the information age.

COMPUTER PROFESSIONALS FOR SOCIAL RESPONSIBILITY
CPSR National Office
P.O. Box 717
Palo Alto, CA 94302
Voice: (415) 322-3778
Internet: cpsr@csli.stanford.edu

National membership organization that conducts activities to protect privacy and civil liberties.

How to Protect Yourself from Computer Criminals

CERT Coordination Center

INCIDENT REPORTING FORM

CERT has developed the following form in an effort to facilitate our interaction with members of the Internet community. We would appreciate your completing the form included below in as much detail as possible. The information is optional, but the more information you can provide, the better we will be able to assist you.

Note that our policy is to keep confidential any information you provide unless we receive your permission to release that information. (See questions 7 and 10 below.)

Please feel free to duplicate any section as required. Please return this form to cert@cert.org. If you are unable to e-mail this form, please send it via FAX. Our FAX telephone number is +1 412-268-6989. Thank you for your cooperation and help.

1. Reporting site information
   Organizational Name (e.g. CERT Coordination Center):
   Domain Name (e.g. cert.org):

2. Your contact information
   Name:
   E-mail address:
   Telephone number:
   FAX number (optional):
   Pager number (optional):
   Home telephone number (for CERT internal use only):

3. Additional contact information (if available)
   Name:
   E-mail address:
   Telephone number:
   FAX number (optional):
   Pager number (optional):
   Home telephone number (for CERT internal use only):

4. Compromised host(s) at your site (one entry per host please)
   Hostname:
   IP address:
   Vendor:
   Hardware:
   OS:
   Version:
   Security patches applied:

5. Please list the other sites compromised that you have notified, and the contact information for each site (one entry per site please)
   Hostname:
      IP address:
      Contact information:
         Name:
         E-mail address:
         Telephone number:
         FAX number (optional):
         Pager number (optional):
         Home telephone number (optional):

6. Please list the other sites compromised that you have not yet notified (one entry per site please)
    Hostname:
    IP address:
    Contact information (if available):
        Name:
        E-mail address:
        Telephone number:
        FAX number (optional):
        Pager number (optional):
        Home telephone number (optional):

7. Would you be willing to contact these sites if CERT provided you the relevant contact information (Yes/No)

   Or, can CERT give your contact information to these sites when we contact them (Yes/No)

8. Incident category (Yes/No)
    Probe:
    Prank:
    Mail Spoofing:
    Breakin:
        Installed Trojan Horse:
        Intruder gained root access:
        NIS (yellow pages) attack:
        NFS attack:
        TFTP attack:
        FTP attack:
        Telnet attack:
        Rlogin or rsh attack:
    Product vulnerability:
    Worm:
    Virus:
    Other (please specify):

9. Are you currently using (Yes/No/Periodically)
    COPS (The Computer Oracle and Password System):
    TCP access control using packet filtering:
    Host access control via modified daemons or wrappers:
    Crack:
    Tripwire:
    Proactive password checkers (e.g. npasswd, passwd+):
    Shadow passwords:
    Other (please specify):

10. Miscellaneous
    Please specify any other incident response team(s) you have contacted
        Team:
        Contact information
            Name:
            E-mail address:
            Telephone number:
            FAX number (optional):
            Pager number (optional):
            Home telephone number (optional):

If you have not contacted another incident response team, could we give them your contact information. (Yes/No)

Please specify any law enforcement agency(ies) you have contacted
        Agency:
        Contact information
            Name:
            E-mail address:
            Telephone number:
            FAX number (optional):
            Pager number (optional):
            Home telephone number (optional):

If you have not contacted any law enforcement agency, could we give them your contact information, if necessary? (Yes/No)

11. Detailed description of incident (e.g. method of intrusion, etc.)

12. What assistance would you like from CERT?

13. Please append any log information or directory listings

CERT is sponsored by the Advanced Research Projects Agency (ARPA). The Software Engineering Institute is sponsored by the U.S. Department of Defense.

How to Protect Yourself from Computer Criminals

Online Resources

Note: Newsgroups and Web sites change frequently. For a comprehensive and up-to-date list of available computer security resource sites, direct your browser to a service such as Yahoo or Webcrawler.

USENET Newsgroups related to computer security:

alt.2600
alt.dcom.telecom
alt.hackers
alt.security.index
alt.security.keydist
alt.security.pgp
alt.security.ripem
alt.security
comp.dcom.telecom
comp.dcom.telecom.tech
comp.org.cpsr.announce
comp.org.cpsr.talk
comp.org.eff
comp.security.announce
comp.security.misc
comp.security.unix
comp.virus
misc.security
sci.crypt

FTP sites for computer security information:

aql.gatech.edu
bellcore.com
cert.org
cipher.com
deimos.cs.uah.edu
eff.org
csua.berkeley.edu
csrc.ncsl.nist.gov
eff.org
etext.org
netcom.com
netsys.com
win.tue.nl
garbo.uwasa.fi
ghost.dsi.unimi.it:
hack-this.pc.cc.cmu.edu
halcyon.com
ripem.msu.edu
rtfm.mit.edu
spy.org
theta.iis.u-tokyo.ac.jp
wimsey.bc.ca

WWW Sites for computer security information:

http://crimelab.com//bugtraq/bugtraq/html
http://cs.purdue.edu/homes/spaf/coast.html
http://cs.purdue.edu/homes/spaf/pcert.html
http://www.eff.org
http://first.org
http://l0pht.com
http://tamsun.tamu.edu/~clm3840/hacking.html
http://www.net23.com
http://www.tnt.uni-hannover.de/stud/hamid.html
http://www.spy.org /Security/Local/News
http://www.phantom.com/~king

Glossary

ACOUSTIC COUPLER: A portable external device used to connect two computers together over a telephone line.

ACCESS: The interaction between a subject and an object that results in a flow of information between the two; also, the act of entering a computer system.

ACCESS CONTROL: Physical and software safeguards preventing unauthorized computer system access.

ACCESS DEVICE CODES: Credit card numbers, telephone authorization numbers and computer passwords.

ACTIVATION PERIOD: Time delay between the time a system is infected with a virus and the actual activation of the virus.

ALPHANUMERIC: Letters and numbers.

ANI: (Automatic Number Identification) Equipment used to identify the calling numbers of a local exchange. (Also known as a Pen Register)

ASCII: (American Standard Code for Information Interchange) An encoding system for converting keyboard characters and instructions into computer binary code.

ATTACK: The act of trying to bypass the security controls of a system.

AUDIT TRAIL: A record of system activity enabling reconstruction, review and examination of the sequence of events leading to an operation, procedure or event, such as an attempted break-in.

AUTHENTICATE: To verify a user's identity.

BACK DOOR: A testing aid left in programs which allows the bypassing of normal security controls. Also known as a trap door.

BACK UP: Copying data to floppy disks as a measure against loss.

BAUD RATE: The speed of data transmission measured in bits per second.

BRUTE FORCE ATTACK: A trial and error method of attempting to break a cipher; usually involves trying every possible combination.

BULLETIN BOARD SYSTEM: (BBS) A computer that is accessible via telephone from another computer.

BINARY: A numbering system which uses only two digits, 0 and 1.

BIT: A binary digit (0 or 1); the smallest piece of computer information.

BOOT: To start up a computer or program. A cold boot involves starting a computer from a main power off configuration, a warm boot involves a running reset.

BOOT INFECTOR: A virus that attaches to the boot sector of a hard or floppy disk.

BOOT SECTOR: The first sector on your hard disk or on a floppy diskette, which is read by the computer when it is booting up.

BOXING: Using multi-frequency tone generators such as a blue box, red box or black box for telephone fraud (see Chapter Two for a list of box types and uses).

BROWSING: The act of searching through computer files without a clear idea of the target information.

BUG: A malfunction in a program or a defect in equipment.

BYTE: Eight-bits comprising a single computer text character.

CALL BACK: Identify verification, sometimes by voice phone call, but usually by automated computer re-call, used to verify an authorized user before allowing dial-in system access.

CHECKSUM: An integrity verifier that calculates the number of bits in each sector, measuring the normal number of bits in a program and matching that against the current number of bits to assist in virus detection.

CHIP: Silicon wafer containing electric circuits used to store millions of bits of information.

CPU: (Central Processing Unit) The brain or master controller of a computer.

CRACKER: Sometimes used to describe a person who engages in computer intrusion, though this term has been superseded by the term hacker. A more common usage is to describe a person who pirates copyrighted software.

CRC: (Cyclic Redundancy Check) A form of error checking used on modem data links to assure that a file has not been corrupted. Occasionally, CRC is used on programs to detect viruses by checking last known byte count with the current byte count. If a virus is attached, the byte count will be higher than normal.

CRT: (Cathode Ray Tube) A computer monitor screen.

DAEMONS: Programs that lay dormant, waiting for the right conditions to occur to invoke them.

DATA DIDDLING: Alteration of computer data.

DATA LEAKAGE: Software or data theft.

DATA STRIPPING: A procedure in which data is split up into small bits of code hidden on different computers.

DEBUG: The process of finding and correcting a malfunction in a computer system or program.

DEMON DIALER: A program that scans hundreds of telephone numbers, searching for those that connect to computers. The program can also make a list of the "hits" found and call back to attempt to crack the passwords.

DES: (Data Encryption Standard) A cryptographic algorithm for the protection of unclassified data.

DIAL-UP: The act of using a computer terminal attached to a telephone line to connect with another computer.

DNR: (Dialed Number Recorder) A DNR captures the electronic impulses traveling over a telephone line as the numbers on a telephone are dialed or pushed. The device records the numbers on a paper tape or on magnetic-media for review, but does not record the content of the communication. A DNR can also record any transmission of the special signaling tones which are used to control communications and their associated billing systems.

DONGLE: A small device that plugs into a computer I/O port, used as a security key for copy protection.

E-MAIL: Acronym for Electronic Mail. Refers to any messages sent from computer to computer (also e-mail; e-Mail).

ENCRYPTION: Encoding information or data so that it cannot be read without the appropriate decoding key.

FAT: File Allocation Table. A list on your hard disk that keeps track of the location of your files.

GLITCH: A malfunction.

HACKER: Generally held to mean a person who intentionally accesses a computer system without proper authorization. Also a term used to describe a computer-literate person who enjoys the nuts and bolts of computing.

HANDLE: A pseudonym used on a bulletin board.

HARD COPY: A paper printout.

HARDWARE: The physical and mechanical components of a computer system.

INTERFACE: A device that connects a computer with a peripheral so that they can communicate with each other.

LOGIC BOMB: A virus that "explodes" and wreaks havoc with computer data when certain conditions are met.

LOOP: A program section that repeats.

LOOP-AROUND-PAIRS: Two telephone company phone numbers used for test purposes. Hackers often use these for free connections.

MODEM: An internal or external device that allows two computers to connect via a telephone line.

NETWORK: A system of computers linked together directly or through telephone lines.

PASSWORD: A protected character string used to authenticate a user's identity.

PENETRATION: The act of successfully bypassing system security.

PERIPHERALS: Extra equipment for the computer that extend its capabilities, such as a printer.

PIGGYBACKING: A method of gaining unauthorized access to a system via another user's legitimate connection; also, a way to gain physical access to a secured area.

PROGRAM: A precise series of instructions written in a computer language, which tells the computer what to do and how to do it.

RABBIT: Piece of software that orders a computer to perform useless tasks repetitively, overwhelming a computer and preventing it from performing any other tasks.

RESIDUAL RISK: The portion of risk that remains after security measures have been applied.

RISK MANAGEMENT: The process of identifying, controlling and eliminating or reducing the possibility of system breaches.

SALAMI TECHNIQUE: Illegally taking small slices of money from a source via computer.

SCAVENGING: A random search through a computer's stored information in an attempt to find valuable or useful data.

SHAREWARE: Computer programs that are made available free of charge, but which require a fee from users for continued use, registration, documentation, upgrades and support.

SHOULDER SURFING: A way to observe computer or telephone numbers as they are entered by looking over a person's shoulder.

SINGLE POINT ACCESS: (SPA) A physical security method for entry into a secured computer area. SPA's are usually the primary way to gain authorized entry, thereby reducing the threat of unauthorized access.

SNIFFER: A program that searches and analyzes a network for specific information.

SPOOFING: An attempt to gain access to a system by posing as an authorized user.

SYSTEM FILES: Main programming files used by the computer operating system.

TRAP DOOR: See Back Door

TRIP WIRE: A program that alerts system operators when access is made into a system. Usually a hacker-catching device set up to monitor for a specific user.

TROJAN HORSE: A virus that masquerades as a legitimate program. Also, a program that captures network passwords into a file for later use by a hacker.

TIME BOMB: See Logic Bomb.

VECTOR: A virus carrier.

VIRUS: An unauthorized piece of computer code attached to a computer program or portions of a computer system that secretly spreads from one computer to another by shared disks and over telephone lines.

WAR DIALING: See Demon Dialer.

WORM: A program that penetrates computers and destroys data.

How to Protect Yourself from Computer Criminals

DON'T BE A VICTIM!

IF YOU'RE LIKE MOST DECENT
AMERICANS YOU'RE WORRIED ABOUT CRIME
AND WHETHER YOU OR SOMEONE YOU LOVE
MAY BECOME A VICTIM.

YOU CAN REDUCE THE RISK TO YOUSELF AND YOUR FAMILY!

ON GUARD! - *How You Can Win the War Against the Bad Guys* - is a valuable, personal weapon in your war against the creeps and crazies out there. *ON GUARD's* "Crime Primers" give you vital information on everything from home security to carjacking and gangs, and will help you avoid becoming a victim. It's information that could even save your life or that of someone you love!

But *ON GUARD* is more! It's a complete guide to organizing your community to reduce - perhaps nearly eliminate crime in your neighborhood. *ON GUARD's* "Citizen Patrol" section shows you what to do and how to do it. Follow *ON GUARD's* recommendations and you and your neighbors will soon be serving as addtional eyes and ears for the police. And that's the last thing a criminal wants — next to jail!

ON GUARD even includes a section of reproduceable "Crime Fighting Forms" you can use to to record suspicious sightings and other information. These paper weapons can play a winning role in your personal war against the bad guys. (The nine forms are also available separately.)

If you're worried about crime you need *ON GUARD* and the practical guidelines and essential information it gives you on the best ways to stay as safe and free from crime as possible in the high-risk 90s!

ON GUARD! - ORDER FORM

Name _____

Address _____

_____

CityState _____ Zip _____

Phone _____

Please send me _____ copies of *ON GUARD* at $17.95 each.

_____ copies of *Crime Fighting Forms* $10.00 ea.

_____ send information about quantity discounts.

*Add $3 s/h first book, $1 for each additional book
or forms set ordered*

My ☐ check ☐ money order for_____ is enclosed.

(WI residents add 5% tax)

Credit Card ☐ Visa ☐ MasterCard

Card # _____ Expiration _____

Name as it appears on card _____

Signature _____

Detach this form and mail to: .

LIMELIGHT BOOKS
PO Box 493
Lake Geneva, WI 53147